STARTING FROM THE CHILD?

STARTING FROM THE CHILD?

Teaching and learning from 4 to 8

JULIE FISHER

Open University Press
Buckingham · Philadelphia

Open University Press
Celtic Court
22 Ballmoor
Buckingham
MK18 1XW

and
1900 Frost Road, Suite 101
Bristol, PA 19007, USA

First Published 1996

A catalogue record of this book is available from the British Library

ISBN   0 335 19556 3 (pb)   0 335 19557 1 (hb)

Library of Congress Cataloging-in-Publication Data
Fisher, Julie. 1950–
     Starting from the child?: teaching and learning from 4 to 8/Julie
Fisher.
        p.   cm.
     Includes bibliographical references and index.
     ISBN 0-335-19556-3 (pb – 0-335-19557-1 (hb)
     1. Early childhood education.   2. Learning, Psychology of.
I. Title.
LB1139.23.F57   1996
372.21–dc20   96–11908
                                                                      CIP

Typeset by Type Study, Scarborough
Printed in Great Britain by St Edmundsbury Press Ltd,
Bury St Edmunds, Suffolk

To Paula,
whose classroom practice inspired this book

CONTENTS

ACKNOWLEDGEMENTS

So much of this book has been influenced by the principles and practice of colleagues with whom I have had the privilege to work. My sincere thanks go to Janet Moyles, who encouraged me to write and opened the doors for me to do so. I am grateful to Keith Postlethwaite, at the University of Reading, who read my early work, took it seriously and gave me the confidence to continue. I am particularly indebted to both Angela Redfern and Carol Boulter who accepted the time-consuming role of 'critical friend' and helped so much to challenge and refine my thinking and writing. My thanks go to my colleagues in the Early Years Curriculum Group who have read and commented on chapters of this book and have been a constant source of inspiration. My thanks also to Tina Bruce for her thought-provoking and supportive comments. I am privileged to be part of the Oxfordshire Early Years Team with Rosemary Knagg, Sue Hale and Kris Gillam, and I am grateful to them for the generous way in which they share their experiences, their ideas, their enthusiasm and their friendship. Finally, my loving thanks to David, who listens endlessly while I rehearse my ideas and gives me the time and space to put them into practice.

1

COMPETENT YOUNG LEARNERS

What children know and can do

Introduction

Before children come to school at the age of 5 they have developed a range of skills, knowledge and understanding at a speed that will never again be repeated in their lives. The years from 0 to 7 are a period in human development when the capacity to learn is, in John Brierley's (1994) words, 'at flood-readiness'. All the evidence shows that, in their early years, young children demonstrate a variety of characteristics which make them natural and successful learners. However, when those same children arrive at school it can be a different story. Children who had been motivated and determined become disillusioned and disaffected (Barrett 1989); children who made sense of things and had begun to form their own personal construct of the world become confused and disorientated (Donaldson 1978); children who posed a thousand and one questions become quiet and uncommunicative (Tizard and Hughes 1984). It seems that schooling can inhibit some of the most prominent characteristics of competent young learners.

Yet quite clearly it is the desire of all teachers to bring about learning, and their efforts to do so and the personal time and commitment they give to their task is not in question (Campbell *et al.* 1993). Despite changes in education policy which, in terms of speed and influence, are unparalleled in the history of the state education system (Pollard *et al.* 1994), most teachers have sustained their commitment to children and to their best interests (Woods 1990). So how can there be such a gap between some children's learning before they begin school and the learning that follows? Is it simply a question of ratios – too many children and not enough teachers – or is the reason more complex? It would seem that at the root of the dichotomy between learning and schooling lies a failure on the part of educationalists in general to learn from those who have been most successful in the teaching and learning process in the child's pre-school years. If more time were spent observing the strategies of children as learners, prior to the constraints of schooling, and more notice taken of the strategies of the significant adults with whom children learn, then there might be more chance of schools mirroring the successes of children's early achievements.

The influence of experience on heredity

If schools are to look more to the learning of children before they reach statutory school age, then it is necessary to understand children's development in those early years. The development of every child is the result of a unique interaction of experience with heredity. While genetic programming determines many of the characteristics displayed by any human being, a variety of environmental influences combine to affect the development of the brain and, consequently, the individual (Shaffer 1993). The balance between these two key factors varies within each child, but the impact of 'nurture' on 'nature' will determine the characteristics which differentiate one child from another and make his or her development unique. Hereditary influence means that given the same set of experiences, one child's abilities will differ from another's, irrespective of the experiences they have. Equally, a child raised in a particular set of circumstances can have their genetic programming nullified and their hereditary advantages erased (Meadows 1993).

Until fairly recently, the emphasis in education had been to make up for the deficits of a poor set of hereditary circumstances (Anning 1991). In the 1960s and 1970s, there was 'a naive belief that compensatory education would serve to combat the known effects of social disadvantage on children's educational achievements'(Anning 1991: 5). While many research studies have now discredited such assumptions, other evidence highlights the negative effects on development of a poor set of environmental factors. Mia Kellmer Pringle (1992: 34), the first director of the National Children's Bureau, identified four human basic needs that have to be met from 'the very beginning of life and continue to require fulfilment – to a greater or lesser extent – throughout adulthood':

- the need for love and security;
- the need for new experiences;
- the need for praise and recognition; and
- the need for responsibility.

Jennie Lindon (1993: 11–12), in her book on child development, also identifies some basic needs of young children:

- the need to be cared for physically;
- the need to be kept safe; and
- the need for emotional well-being.

All of these needs have to be met by the caring adult if children are to thrive and make the most of their developmental opportunities. Recent research cited by the Carnegie Corporation of New York (1994) provides substantial evidence that a *lack* of certain experiences, and inappropriate or impoverished environments in the early stages of learning, may have long-lasting detrimental effects on the development of children. The report, which drew on research that illuminates the workings of the nervous system, highlights the critical importance of the first 3 years of life. The research resulted in five key findings, which are of profound significance to all those concerned with the development and education of young children:

- brain development that takes place before age one is more rapid and extensive than previously realised;
- brain development is much more vulnerable to environmental influence than was ever suspected;
- the influence of early environment on brain development is long lasting;
- the environment affects not only the number of brain cells and number of connections among them, but also the way these connections are 'wired';
- there is new scientific evidence for the negative impact of early stress on brain function.

(Carnegie Corporation 1994: 7–9)

These findings give a clear rationale for creating environments that offer experiences sensitive to the needs of young children and appropriate to their development, because the results of these experiences – good or bad – stay with children for ever. The fact that the effects of early experiences appear to be cumulative only adds to the need to safeguard the environmental influences which determine the development of all young children:

> an adverse environment can compromise a young child's brain function and overall development, placing him or her at greater risk of developing a variety of cognitive, behavioral, and physical difficulties. In some cases these effects may be irreversible.
>
> (Carnegie Corporation 1994: xiii)

What do young children learn?

Given an appropriate environment in which they thrive, what is it that young children are learning? Shaffer (1993: 5) claims that 'we change in response to the environments in which we live'. In particular, such change is in response to the actions and reactions of the people around us. We behave in new ways because of our observations of, and interactions with, important people in our lives and are affected by the events we experience. Young children come to make sense of their world by observing, imitating, investigating and exploring. They learn skills, strategies and concepts which enable them to understand and be understood.

Important *skills* are learned as a result of establishing patterns of behaviour which ultimately become automatic. Young children repeat movements or actions time after time in order to become expert and succeed at the goals which they have set themselves. Skills usually develop in the course of activities which children see as being worthwhile and which give them the motivation to continue, sometimes through failure after failure, to succeed. Children are motivated by the response of others, particularly their parent or carer, and this response sustains them through the frustrations of learning to stand alone, throw a ball towards someone else or make their desire for food clearly understood.

In the course of learning skills, children develop their own peculiar set of *strategies* for trying out, rehearsing or repeating what they have done. Some children prefer to look and think before they act. Some try and try again until something comes right. Some prefer to imitate, some to instigate. Some ask questions and others wait for answers. Whatever strategies are developed, they are tailor-made by each child – they are chosen because they serve the child's individual purpose and because they work. These strategies become part of the characteristics of the child as a learner and are the basis of all strategies that will be adopted if the child is left to learn alone.

The understandings or *concepts* that children learn are generally arrived at through a process of abstraction of the principles which underpin a number of different experiences. Children come to understand about size, colour, the past or the seasons through a variety of first-hand experiences which lead them to see and understand the conceptual links between one experience and another. In this way, children become able to generalize abstract principles from concrete experiences. It is almost impossible to rush this transition from concrete to abstract because if children are forced to establish connections, then it is likely that they will make inappropriate ones (Brierley 1994). We know that children *do* make the wrong 'connections' and that, once made, these misunderstandings – or alternative under-standings – can take a great deal of unlearning. The work of Wynne Harlen, Roger Osborne and others reveals that children have views about a variety of topics and that they are very often different from the views of 'experts'. However, to children, they remain 'sensible, useful views' (Harlen 1985: 76) and can remain uninfluenced or be influenced in quite unanticipated ways by teaching. The views that children hold are a result of their personal endeavours to construct their own meaning for, and understanding of, the experiences they have had (Postlethwaite 1993). They work for the child who has con-structed them and, since they serve the child's purpose quite well, they may not readily be displaced by the explanation of someone else, especially as these explanations are often more complex than their own.

Readiness for learning

Inherent in beliefs about the competences of young children is an atti-tude towards the concept of 'readiness' for learning. If children are viewed as competent young learners, then it follows that they have predispositions to learn from their earliest days and, as such, are ready for learning from birth (and, some would say, before). The conse-quence of this view is that children are never *not* ready to learn and the notion of children 'emerging' into literacy (Hall 1987), numeracy (Hughes 1986) and so on, assumes engagement in concepts which at one time would have been deemed inappropriate for young minds. But the work of Donaldson (1978), Bruner (1986), Hughes (1986) and others has encouraged the view that children are ready for learning if learning is adapted to the intellectual proclivities of children (Watson 1996).

Once more we are drawn to the behaviours of parents and carers who appear to make these adaptations instinctively. Parents, it would seem, adapt naturally to their child's intellectual tendencies, attribu-ting consciousness and intentionality to their child's actions from the very beginning of his or her life (Stern 1985). When parents talk to their child, they do so as if expecting a response, often long before the child seems capable of giving one. In this way, suggests Watson (1996), children's early learning is aided in spontaneous and incidental ways by older and more experienced members of their community, who give structure to the child's 'earliest, hesitant inclinations to explore the world'.

A child is ready to learn when his or her cognitive disposition and what is to be taught are matched. Parents may make this match instinctively knowing, as they do, so much about the body of beliefs, expectations and assumptions which their child brings to a learning situation. Teachers do not have the benefit of sharing each child's learning history and one of the most complex challenges of teaching is to become as knowledgeable as possible about the cognitive dispositions of a large number of children in any one class.

Much of the influence of Jean Piaget stemmed from his view that children progress through various stages of development which determine their current level of skills and competence. Readiness for learning, he believed, depended on each child's developmental stage, and progress from one stage to the next could not be rushed. This view of development influenced many teachers to adopt a relatively passive role in children's progress (Darling 1994). Teachers planned activities that reflected the notion of readiness with titles such as 'pre-reading', 'pre-number' and so on. The role of the teacher was to bring children to a state of readiness to engage fully in significant skills or concepts and children were taken through a whole range of early stages of learning in preparation for their arrival at the next stage of development. Piaget's notion of readiness was ultimately challenged by a number of researchers, most notably Margaret Donaldson (1978), who believed that children should be actively encouraged to move towards the 'disembedded' thinking which characterizes learning in schools. The work of Lev Vygotsky (1978) has also been highly influential in this debate about readiness. Vygotsky believed that instead of matching teaching to existing development, teaching had to proceed in advance of development in order to challenge and extend children's maturing functions. He believed that learning comes before development when progress is stimulated and guided by the expertise of others. This notion of readiness places the emphasis not so much on *when* to teach, but rather *how* and *what* to teach.

The characteristics of successful early learning

Young children may be inexperienced learners, but their competence should no longer be underestimated. Modern technology has made it possible to investigate the very beginnings of human thinking, and researchers have documented critical development in the pre- and post-natal months of life (Carnegie Corporation 1994). From the beginning, humans demonstrate intention-directed behaviour (Blenkin and Kelly 1987). They are both intellectually and interpersonally engaged, or predisposed to be so, much earlier than previous theories allowed (Watson 1996). The young child is clearly emerging cognitively, linguistically, physically, socially and emotionally and – most significantly – this critical development occurs when the child is receiving no formal education. Children have the capacity to draw conclusions about the world when the knowledge that they need has not been formally taught to them.

Given an environment in which they are cared for and in which they can thrive, young children display a range of competences which make their early learning dramatically successful:

- Young children display *motivation* and *determination*. They want to succeed, they want to conquer, because the world is an exciting, stimulating place and there is just so much to find out about.
- Young children demonstrate *persistence* and *perseverance*. The desire to find out and to do is so strong that children will try over and over again – through failure after failure – to succeed.
- Young children develop personal *skills* and *strategies* which work for them in their quest to understand the world. These strategies are chosen instinctively and fulfil children's purposes for the particular task in hand.
- Young children have developed *understandings* and sometimes *mis-understandings*. Each piece of knowledge acquired, each small piece of sense that is made, fits into each child's personal cognitive jigsaw.

The construction of this personal cognitive jigsaw has many parallels with the construction of the traditional wooden puzzle. At first, the pieces of the cognitive jigsaw are picked seemingly at random. Sometimes the piece fits straight away; sometimes it is turned round and round – with astonishing patience – before the fit is finally made. Sometimes the piece is turned round and round and a fit is made and only subsequent pieces show the piece to be in the wrong place. Sometimes the piece is turned round and round, does not quite fit but is jammed in anyway because it is more satisfying to have reached a solution than to have to start again.

It is the skill of the educator to be aware of the pieces of the jigsaw that the child already has in place and whether or not they have been fitted together correctly. If they have not, then supporting the child to review the construction of their cognitive jigsaw is as delicate and difficult an operation as persuading the child to select an alternative piece of wooden puzzle. The 'teacher' – whether an adult or another child – needs to be informative without being imposing. Imposition simply leads to the learner becoming confused and disaffected. Confusion arises because the links between the pieces have been made by the teacher and not by the learner. Disaffection occurs because the initiative has been taken away from the learner and the construction no longer makes personal sense.

The expertise of the child's first educators

We have seen that young children's early learning is not only the result of their own predispositions to learning, but also the result of interactions with significant others in their family and their community at large. It is important to appreciate the strategies that parents use which make them such successful educators, very often without realizing it.

1 Crucially, of course, most parents *love* and *care* about their children and have a genuine interest in their actions, ideas and development. Parents may be very busy, be feeling under the weather, be preoccupied with other things – but the bond between them and their children surfaces under all manner of stresses and strains to reassure the child of the strength of the relationship between them (Sylva and Lunt 1982).

2 Parents *operate in the real world*. They talk to their children in kitchens and bathrooms, they take them to shops and playgrounds and cinemas, they eat with them in front of the television or in McDonald's. Parents and their children are surrounded by a cacophony of visual, aural and tactile stimuli – sights and sounds which constantly fascinate children and cause them to ask what, how and why?

3 Parents are often in a *one-to-one situation*, or at least one and a very small group situation, when these questions are asked. Although every parent knows that feeling of being asked one question too many, research into the interactions between children and their parents and children and their teachers (Tizard and Hughes 1984; Wells 1986) reveals that however brief – not to say curt – parental responses might be, parents still interact far more frequently with their children than the teacher with her twenty, thirty or forty children. In the home, children are able to talk about a range of topics, to initiate and sustain conversations and to ask questions endlessly, and all of these factors make the home 'a powerful learning environment' (Tizard and Hughes 1984).

4 In these situations, parents usually *respond to* rather than *initiate* learning. The child wants to know, wants to know what to do, wants to know what to do next – and the parent is there to supply the appropriate piece of the jigsaw, there to support and to facilitate the developing learner.

Studying children and their parents can offer those of us in formal education many lessons about effective early learning. It is so important that teachers draw on the expertise of parents and enable them to inform and to go on informing the school about their child. It can be too easy to pay lip service to the notion of a partnership with parents, but teachers should not forget that it is *they* who join the already established learning partnership which exists between the parent and their child.

How do young children learn?

While it is possible to identify the learning characteristics of young children, it is altogether more difficult to try and understand exactly how they learn. There is no conclusive evidence on this subject, although there have been a number of influential theories over the course of the last two centuries. The theories have grown and developed one from the other and many have, at some point or another, had an impact on the way in which children have been educated (see Entwhistle 1987; Wood 1988; Anning 1991).

Young children learn by being active

Any personal study of young children reveals almost non-stop activity in the quest for skills, strategies and understandings. But the work of Jean Piaget and other contemporary theorists of child development emphasizes that 'being active' does not necessarily mean 'moving around'. Being active means that young children *engage* with experiences, actively (as opposed to passively) bringing their existing knowledge and understanding to bear on what is currently under investigation. Being active is what causes children both physically and cognitively to construct their own view of the world, to personalize the experience and to apply it in ways which make sense to them as individuals (Bruner and Haste 1987).

Young children learn by organizing their own learning experiences

The work of Chris Athey at the Froebel Institute has provided a new framework for studying the patterns of children's behaviour as they learn. These early patterns of behaviour (or schemas, as they are defined) are seen in babies, and become more complex and more numerous as a child develops. By becoming familiar with these behaviours, the observer comes to realize that actions are not performed in isolation but are one of a set of experiences coordinated by the child (Nutbrown 1994). Athey, in her book *Extending Thought in Young Children* (1990), illustrates how such patterns can be represented in children's play, their thinking and their language. Once in tune with these categories of behaviour, adults have a valuable framework for observing children's actions. Schemas are a way of understanding the learning behaviours of children and, as such, give adults and educators an appreciation of what is currently interesting and absorbing the child. 'It is through schemas, and the fitting of content to different schematic threads, that children's own construction of reality and subsequent continuity can be identified' (Nutbrown 1994: 36).

Young children learn by using language

The language development of young children is a staggering phenomenon. The increase in young children's vocabulary and their growing capacity to use language for a range of purposes is powerful evidence of an innate drive to make meaning and to communicate. The research of Gordon Wells and his team on the Bristol Language Study concluded that in the early stages, children's linguistic systems are more or less in place and a basic vocabulary of several thousand words is acquired. From that point on, however, what is learned and the order in which it is learned becomes 'progressively more dependent on experience – on having opportunities to hear the relevant functions, meanings, and structure used appropriately and to use them oneself' (Wells 1986: 32).

Wells sees language as a code to be cracked, but that before a child attempts this, he or she has already become familiar with the code in use. Language development relies on children hearing and using language in meaningful interactions. In order to work out for themselves how language is organized, children need the collaborative help of 'conversational partners' who 'provide clear and relevant feedback', enabling the children to evaluate the appropriateness of their current hypotheses. This does not mean that it is necessarily best for adults to overtly teach children the use of language. As in other areas of their development, children construct their own internal models of language and, rather than adults teaching children, 'it is children who teach adults how to talk in such a way as to make it easy for them to learn' (Wells 1986: 48).

Language provides not only a means of acting on the world, but also for reflecting on that action in an attempt to understand it (Harlen 1985). Piaget argued that language is a 'medium', a method of representation within which thought takes place. Vygotsky, on the other hand, believed that speech transforms the way in which children learn, think and understand and is, therefore, a 'tool' of thought (Wood 1988). The theories of Jerome Bruner draw and build on the work of both Piaget and Vygotsky. His assertion is that the internalization of language is an instrument of thought and that the very young child uses language 'almost as an extension of pointing'. All of these theories depend on the understanding that thought, action and language are inextricably bound together in children's development. The successful development of all three is dependent on experiences being embedded in what is meaningful for the child.

Young children learn by interacting with others

Children may well be active learners in a highly individualistic sense, but they construct their personal meanings within the framework of a social and cultural context (Wood 1988). The young child is a social being, playing, talking and living alongside others, watching what they do and imitating them, questioning what is seen and responding to questioning, drawing on the knowledge and expertise of others to interpret and make meaning of experiences (Richards and Light 1986; Wells 1986; Dunn 1988). Everything that young children learn is influenced by the culture in which they grow up and the community in which they live. The writing of Vygotsky emphasized the significance of social contexts for learning, whereby adults – or other more expert members of the community – help children to acquire skills and understandings which they might not accomplish, or accomplish less speedily, alone. Vygotsky refers to the gap between what children are able to do alone and what they can achieve with help as the 'zone of proximal development'; in other words, 'the distance between the actual developmental level as determined by independent problem solving and the level of potential development as determined through problem solving under adult guidance or in collaboration with more capable peers' (Vygotsky 1978: 86).

The work of Wood *et al.* (1976) extends this notion, adopting the metaphor 'scaffolding' to describe the guidance and interactional support given by the adult or expert until the child is able to take over tasks for him or herself. In this model of learning, children are not passively absorbing the strategies of the adult, but take an active, inventive role (Smith 1993), reconstructing the tasks through their own understanding while the adult or educator provides what Bruner (1985) describes as a 'vicarious form of consciousness'.

Implications for classroom practice

What then are the implications for classroom practice of the issues which this chapter has raised? What strategies do teachers need to consider if they are to build on what is known about how young children learn?

Young children learn by being active

If young children learn naturally by being active and engaging in a range of exploratory experiences, then the primary responsibility of the school is to plan opportunities which facilitate and support these instinctive strategies. Children need opportunities to engage with a range of materials and stimuli. They need time and space to explore, investigate and question. They need a range of play experiences and appropriate resources of good quality. They need, in other words, a learning environment that offers concrete experiences which are relevant, meaningful and worthy of active involvement. If children are to continue their struggle to make sense of the world, then the world must be worth the struggle. Clearly, before children start school, the incentive and motivation to learn have been sufficient. It is up to schools to make children's new learning environment equally worthwhile. Some teachers have been concerned that supporting this development demands the construction of individual learning programmes. But although the development of each child is unique, there are many similarities between how children in general develop and, therefore, many ways in which teachers can and should plan for children's learning as part of a small or larger group (see Chapter 6).

Young children learn by organizing their own learning experiences

Athey (1990) reminds us that in order to tap into the personal constructs of the child, teachers need to focus on the underlying processes of their thinking and cognition. When teachers are concerned with the sense which children are making of their own learning, then this provides a rich source for planning and development. Observation and appreciation of children's schemas can offer teachers a starting point for planning experiences which capture children's current interests and absorptions. If a child is focusing on a trajectory schema – a fascination with things moving or flying through the air (see Bartholomew and Bruce 1993, for further definitions of schema) – then 'he or she needs to be provided with a range of interesting and stimulating experiences which extend thinking along that particular path'(Nutbrown 1994: 15). When children are absorbed by something in this way, it is far more productive for teachers to go with and plan for that interest. Starting from the child becomes increasingly difficult when there is an external curriculum to be taught (Chapter 3 will address this issue in depth); however, teachers who believe in working with rather than against the interests of children will make time to observe and record the ways in which they organize their own learning experiences. Nutbrown notes that those who become interested in children's schema development soon realize that children will pursue their schemas, whether adults like it or not!

Young children learn by using language

The work of Margaret Donaldson (1978) demonstrates the importance of young children's experiences being embedded in contexts which are meaningful to them. Her work, and that of researchers studying the relationship between language development in the home and at school, emphasizes the importance of the contexts in which adults and children have shared experiences in common from which to draw shared meanings (Anning 1991). Edwards and Mercer (1987) claim that the establishment of mutual understanding and shared meanings is something with which teachers must also be concerned. They suggest that the point at which education commonly fails, is when 'incorrect assumptions are made about shared knowledge, meaning and interpretations' (p. 60). Teachers and pupils need to share a 'common knowledge' about the discourse which forms the basis for classroom communication in order for the learning that comes from interaction to be most effective.

Children use language to learn and, therefore, classrooms must give them opportunities to use language in a variety of ways. It is language which affords young children the means of making sense of their experiences and of internalizing their actions. In order to capitalize on the power of language to influence both thought and action, classroom experiences must encourage talk as a key process through which young children learn. Talking something through, either alone or with others, is an important way of grasping new ideas, understanding concepts or clarifying feelings and perceptions. Young children need opportunities for discussion, for explanation, for description, for narration and for speculation. In classrooms where talk is recognized as a powerful and natural medium for learning, young children are able to make meaning of what is new in terms of what is familiar. Through their talk, they create a new context which is personal to them and one which relates to their own experiences (Britton 1970).

Young children learn by interacting with others

If learning is socially constructed, then teachers clearly have a critical role in classrooms, a role at one time devalued by misunderstandings about the nature of 'child-centredness' and 'discovery learning' (Blenkin and Kelly 1987). It is the skilled intervention of teachers which moves children from their present to their future potential.

Interactions with children must facilitate this progress through Vygot-sky's 'zone of proximal development' and teachers must arrange things, says Athey (1990), so that knowledge is actively constructed and not simply copied. Teachers need to plan classroom time so that they have regular conversations with children. These conversations need to be designed to find out what a child already knows and under-stands (see Chapter 2), or to support, through questioning or answer-ing questions, the child's current thinking. Such conversations need to be planned and should not happen incidentally. To bring this about, teaching time needs to be organized so that adults can focus on their planned learning objectives and not be distracted by unre-lated interruptions (Chapter 4).

Other children are also part of this social construct, and teachers have to look at 'the context in which learning takes place in schools as well as at the nature of specific learning tasks' (Pollard and Tann 1993). The topic of children working together and learning together is discussed fully in Chapter 6, but there is growing evidence of the importance of peer tutoring in classroom contexts – whether teachers plan for it or not (see, for example, Forman and Cazden 1985). Effec-tive teaching acknowledges the role of *all* those who have knowledge and understandings to contribute to the development of individual learners.

Conclusion

When children start school, they are already competent learners. Competence evolves from the fusion of children's natural predisposi-tion to learn and the appropriateness of the support they receive while learning. This chapter has suggested that those responsible for the more formal stages of children's education need to look to the charac-teristics of children's successful early learning environments in order to develop models of teaching which will lead to the continuation of effective learning throughout the child's school life. In the next chapter, we examine how teachers establish the range of competences which children bring to school and how teachers come to find out what children already know about and can do.

2

CONVERSATIONS AND OBSERVATIONS

Establishing a baseline

Introduction

If we acknowledge that children bring to school certain skills, knowledge and understandings, then a key task of the teacher is to identify precisely what it is that children already know and can do in order to build on their existing competences. This immediately defines the classroom experiences of both teachers and children. If children already know and can do a range of things, then it puts the teacher in the role of learner alongside her class. The teacher must find out the extent of children's competences to ensure that the planned curriculum is appropriate to this particular class and its individual members. This leads to planning which is tailor-made for each child because the foundations for learning are unique. Each child has his or her own personal history of experiences which will determine not only what they need to learn next, but how they will do so most effectively.

Establishing the starting points for children's educational experiences is not a task which takes place only when a child begins school. Teachers need to establish the starting points for children's learning throughout their schooling as part of the ongoing cycle of teaching and learning. All too often the planned curriculum establishes its starting points from what has been taught in school, and what a previous teacher has 'covered'. However, children continue to learn in and from a range of contexts that are nothing to do with the classroom, and it is always necessary to discover what knowledge and understanding children bring with them from their previous life experiences in order to plan a curriculum which matches their current learning needs.

The teacher as learner

Placing themselves in the role of learner, teachers make assessments of children's knowledge, skills and understandings before finalizing the planning of an appropriate curriculum. All too often, assessment is seen as the end of the teaching process, undertaken to discover whether children have learnt what was planned. But there is a critical place for assessment at the start of the cycle of teaching and learning, when teachers find out what children already know and can do so that the next experiences planned are relevant and meaningful. Assessment is a tool which begins and ends successful teaching. At the beginning it establishes what is currently known and at the end it establishes what has been learnt as the result of the planned curriculum. This chapter is concerned with the two key ways in which teachers establish, at the beginning of the teaching and learning cycle, what children already know and can do. The first strategy is to have *conversations* with those who know about the child as a learner. The second strategy is to make *observations* of the child in action as a learner.

Having conversations

Teachers need to have informative conversations with a range of people who have knowledge of the child as a learner. These conversations need to inform the teacher:

• what interests the child;
• what motivates the child to learn;
• how the child perceives him or herself as a learner;
• what the child already knows about and can do; and
• what the child would like to know about or do.

   Having a range of conversations gives teachers a range of perspectives on each child and these perspectives help to form a rounded and balanced picture of the learner. Each perspective is valid and needs to be valued, and each contributes something fresh to the teacher's understanding of the child and their needs. Putting together this profile is rather like undertaking a detective investigation as the teacher gathers together the pieces of the evidence which she needs in order to make hypotheses and judgements upon which to proceed in her work.

Conversations with children

Conversations with children – where children do most of the talking – provide teachers with evidence of children's responses to learning and to experiences. They offer the children's version of what they have just experienced – not the *intended* learning outcomes, but the *actual* learning outcomes. They reveal how children have approached an activity, what they found interesting, what strategies they used for making sense of the world and where any misunderstandings might lie. Such conversations give teachers hard evidence of children's development. When children have to put into words what they have done and learnt, and how they have gone about it, then their thoughts and language provide teachers with clear evidence on which to build the next stages of learning. At this age, oral evidence provides more detailed and reliable information than recorded evidence. The capacity of young children to think and understand far outstrips their capacity to interpret that knowledge and understanding in recorded form and written evidence can present a very limited version of their experiences. The very act of articulating ideas and understandings reveals a wealth of information about the child's learning: what they have understood, what they have misunderstood, what skills they have used and what they have enjoyed. Conversations with children offer the teacher a marvellous assessment opportunity as they reveal needs *and* interests, and can be a critical moment in the cycle of teaching and learning.

It is crucial that conversations are meaningful to the child and that the teacher genuinely wants to find out about what she is asking about. Questions should demand answers which the teacher does not already know, otherwise the questioning technique is simply being used as a checking device, to discover whether children are paying attention or not. Young children are all too aware of whether teachers' questions are genuine. This is scathingly exemplified by 5-year-old Sonnyboy, who responded to his teacher's meaningless questioning with a question of his own: 'Why do you keep asking the kids questions when you knows all the answers? Like ... like ... what colour is it then? You can see for yourself it's red ... so why do you keep asking them?' (Cousins 1990: 30).

Skilful, open-ended questioning leads children to share their own thoughts, ideas and perceptions with the teacher and teaches the teacher something more about the child. When young children record what they know or understand, then the evidence of their learning may be far more limited. It can be limited by a child's capacity to record, to write or draw what they have done or understood. It can be limited by a child's understanding of the task or the worksheet. It can be limited by the page or sheet which simply requires that boxes are filled in and leaves no space for the child's original thought or interpretation. Since schools have been subjected to inspection by the Office for Standards in Education (Ofsted), there has been great concern among early years practitioners that evidence of children's achievements must be in written form. It is widely believed that a child's picture, model or talk does not carry the same weight as a piece of writing, and worksheets are more and more in evidence. This is a worrying trend. A child is far more complex a learner than can ever be evidenced by a worksheet. If we want evidence of what a child knows and understands, then we must look at the richest and most powerful evidence available – the child's own actions and the child's own words.

Conversation with parents

Conversations with parents add to the developing picture of the child as a learner. Parents bring their knowledge of the child in a variety of contexts which the teacher may never be privileged to see. A good case for home visiting is made when teachers recount what they have learnt from seeing the child in the surroundings of their own home, and how relationships change when parents meet teachers on their own territory (see Edwards and Redfern 1988, for a very practical account of the development of partnerships with parents).

Conversations with parents should take place before the child starts school, when the child starts school and after the child has started school. These conversations need to acknowledge the expertise which parents have about their own children and the understanding which parents have about their children's needs and interests. If teachers want to know about children in order to build on the children's existing abilities, then part of that knowledge comes from parents, and teachers can acknowledge this by providing a range of opportunities to listen to and record parental knowledge, attitudes and ideas. These conversations should not take place just at the beginning of the child's school or class experience. Parents continue to have a fresh, different and crucial perspective on their child's development, their attitude to school and learning and their growing skills and competences. We all know that children can behave as two different beings – both in attitude and approach – from home to school, and it is an impoverished profile of the child as a learner which only takes account of the child in the context of school:

> It would not make sense to try to educate a child without taking account of the most significant people in his/her environment, and trying to work with them. It is through the home context that school becomes meaningful, or not, to a family.
>
> (Bruce 1991: 15)

Much of the following material about parental partnership is taken from the Oxfordshire Education Department's (1996) *Curriculum Matters* series on early years. It looks, in practical ways, at strategies for developing effective relationships with parents and carers.

Before children start school
From the time a family first makes contact with a school, or a school first makes contact with a family, there are opportunities for a dynamic partnership to be established. To enable this to develop, schools could offer some of the following:

- an invitation to use the toy library and/or book library;
- invitations to school events such as assembly, performances, fairs and other special occasions;
- invitations to share amenities such as a wild area, hall, family room, swimming pool.

These informal contacts are invaluable for building confidence between parents, children and the school staff. From such beginnings a more formal induction process can evolve naturally.

Parental entitlement
Schools need to think carefully about how they help *all* parents and children to feel valued and welcomed at the beginning of their school life. Teachers may want to consider the extent to which, in their school, parents have an entitlement to:

- share their greater knowledge of their child, prior to entry, and throughout their time in school;
- enter a partnership with the school which takes account of various cultures, languages and styles;
- sufficient time and opportunity for regular formal and informal communication with the school;
- dialogue with teachers where parents' opinions and ideas are valued and have influence;
- communicate their aspirations for their child;
- comment on and contribute to the records of their child's achievements in all areas of development.

Parental partnership
In order to facilitate a partnership with parents, schools may want to initiate many or all of the following strategies:

- visit families at home (remembering that some parents may prefer to meet in school);
- design an entry profile for completion by parents and children;

- use photographs and/or a video camera to record everyday and special events;
- communicate school aims and routines using visual material;
- share school activities by making a range of small books;
- use home/school diaries, either audiotaped or written (community languages should be used where possible);
- organize a range of times during the day and evening for meetings and appointments;
- organize a creche for younger children;
- arrange for someone at meetings who can speak the community languages;
- enable an outreach worker/key worker/friend to attend with a family if support is required;
- adopt a flexible and imaginative response to the needs of families and the community;
- respect the variety and depth of information which parents convey about their children;
- recognize the diversity of values within the wider school community;
- give parents opportunities to express their own expectations of the school;
- give parents opportunities to express their hopes for their child both inside and apart from school;
- give parents opportunities to express their own fears and misgivings;
- ask parents to describe
    their child's interests
    their child's likes and dislikes
    what their child can do
    the history of their child's experiences
    their child's health
    their child's friends
    what is special to their child
    people who are important to their child
    what their child hopes to do at school
    what their child fears about school;
- share the strengths and achievements of their child at school;
- discuss ways in which parents and the school can work together to support the child's learning.

Conversations with parents can benefit all parties concerned. It benefits teachers because of their increased knowledge of the child, it benefits parents by making them genuine partners in their child's learning and it benefits children, who see home and school as mutually interested in their education.

Conversations with other adults

The third group of people with whom the teacher needs to have con-versations is those other adults who have experience of the child as a learner outside the context of the home and before starting school. Playgroup leaders, child-minders, day care workers all may have worked with the child in a very different context than the home. They will have experience of the child in settings which require social adjustments and institutional expectations. These workers will have experience of the child in varied learning situations and will have much to contribute to the picture of the child as a learner. There are many excellent examples of early years practitioners who have worked hard to establish links with all the agencies who have knowledge of, and concern for, the pre-school child. Many of these relationships are built at local level. For example, individual teachers, health visitors, outreach workers and play group leaders have established networks that ensure that the best interests of the young child are met through a regular exchange of knowledge about the child and their family. Such information is invaluable to the reception class teacher who has a basis from which to begin – or indeed to continue – a profile of the child and their achievements. The more that early years practitioners talk to each other and come to understand and appreciate each other, the greater will be their strength in presenting a united front to cam-paign for the rights of young children and their education.

Making observations

The other key mechanism for finding out what children already know and can do is by observing them while they are in action as learners. Children are naturally active learners (Bruce 1987; EYCG 1992), so it is imperative that to learn about them teachers should watch them in action. If our objective is to find out the full range of what children know and understand, then this cannot be achieved by limiting the observations that are made. Children should be observed while they are engaged in a range of activities, both teacher-initiated and child-initiated, which should occur:

- in familiar learning contexts;
- in an environment which encourages confidence and builds self-esteem;
- alongside a range of peers;
- when a child is working with an adult;
- when the child is working independently; and
- at different times of the day and week.

Teacher-initiated and child-initiated activity

Observations of children need to encompass activities that have been self-initiated and activities that have been initiated by the teacher. Self-initiated activity gives children opportunities to make choices and decisions of their own. It enables children to demonstrate their independence, as well as their social skills, in choosing to work with others. Self-initiated activity gives children control over situations, and sometimes their peers, and puts children in rare positions of classroom power (Warham 1993). Appropriately resourced and supported, child-initiated activity can bring about some of the most creative and innovative learning in the classroom (Whitehead 1993).

Teacher-initiated activity is equally important. A key purpose of education is to broaden the range of children's knowledge and experience and this is appropriately planned for by the specialist practitioner. In teacher-initiated activities, there are opportunities for children to work with a variety of adults and peers for a range of purposes. Children engage in ideas and action which are new to them and which they may not have discovered for themselves.

Both kinds of experience – teacher-initiated and child-initiated – are important and one without the other will not give children sufficiently broad and balanced opportunities for learning. Equally, one without the other will not give the adult a sufficiently rounded picture of the child as a learner. Example 1 illustrates the importance of knowing as much about the young learner as possible.

Familiar learning contexts

If teachers are to observe children in contexts in which they will be at their best, then it is necessary to establish an environment which is familiar and which builds on the best of children's pre-school experiences. We have already seen in Chapter 1 how successful a child's first learning environment is. But as well as the home situation, many children have other valuable pre-school experiences which can give an insight into the kind of educational environment that will stimulate and involve them as learners. The ways in which children of 3 and 4 years learn so successfully does not change dramatically with the blowing out of five candles! Teachers in this country are fortunate to have excellent examples of pre-school provision on which to model their own practice. If children are secure and confident in a learning environment that encourages choice, decision making and a curriculum based on exploration and play, then surely this is the learning environment which children should meet when they start school.

Example 1: Building a balanced profile

A student on teaching practice was building a very thorough profile of a
6-year-old boy in her class and was using it to try and establish why his
behaviour was antagonistic and why she had such difficulty in engaging
and sustaining his interest. When we looked at the profile together, it
became clear that she had observed the child when engaged in activities which she had initiated. Although she was aware that he 'liked
making things', she had not observed his involvement in self-selected
tasks from which she might make judgements about future, more
appropriate planning. For the next few days, she observed the child
engaged in self-initiated activities and soon found that he did indeed
enjoy making things, particularly with construction kits, and was very
skilful at it. Talking with him about his models, she found that he was
very knowledgeable about aeroplanes and regularly visited air shows
with his father. When working on his self-selected tasks, she was amazed
to find that he was cooperative and supportive to other children who
worked alongside him. The student learnt that there was another side to
this child. She saw a side of him that, observing him in directed situations, she might never have seen. By combining her knowledge of the
child in both situations, she was able to plan teacher-initiated tasks
which incorporated the positive aspects she had learnt about the child
through her observations of his self-selected activity.

A discussion of how to marry the demands of an early years curriculum with the legal requirements of the National Curriculum will be
dealt with in Chapter 3, but here I would simply contend that for children and for teachers, a classroom environment modelled on the best
of nursery practice is the most appropriate environment for 5-year-
olds as well as 4-year-olds. Indeed, my own experiences of working
alongside some highly gifted junior teachers is that good nursery practice *remains* the underpinning for effective teaching at any stage in a
child's primary education.

An environment that encourages confidence and builds self-esteem

Confidence and self-esteem are built in a myriad of ways and many of
these have already been mentioned in this chapter. Children's self-
image is enhanced when their culture and traditions are respected
and acknowledged by the teacher and used in the planning of an
appropriate curriculum. Young children's feelings and attitudes are

Example 2: Responding to children's work

A teacher of a vertically grouped class of Year 1 and Year 2 children wanted to develop the children's ability to evaluate their own work. She wanted them to move away from relying on her for decisions about whether what they had done was 'enough' or 'good enough'. She suspected that this reliance stemmed from the fact that, as she had set the tasks, the children believed that only she could judge the quality of the results. So she decided to change the entire way in which she introduced activities to the class. After the initial discussion and the introduction of the activity, she would ask the children what they thought was important in completing the task. She supported the children in thinking through the processes, the skills, the knowledge and the understandings they might need to demonstrate in the course of the activity and what the outcomes might be. They then decided which of these were the most important and these were recorded on a large sheet of paper and left pinned to the wall. At the end of the session, the children would gather with their work and then review their own efforts against the criteria which the class had compiled collectively. In this way, the children were developing their personal responses to their own work and in the process were being challenged to use their initiative and to take responsibility for their learning and its outcomes. The teacher reported growing confidence and self-esteem as the children became involved in setting their own criteria for achievement in this way.

crucial to their achievements in all aspects of life and yet there is little recognition of this in recent national documentation. It is important that those of us working in the field of early childhood education fight to preserve the affective elements of the curriculum and to sustain the social and emotional aspects of children's development. Rosemary Roberts (1995a) recently examined how children's feelings affect their attitudes to school and showed how self-esteem can be the key to effective teaching and learning. As teachers we can help to build self-esteem through the response that we give to children and to their attitudes, ideas and efforts. This does not mean heaping them with empty praise, but supporting them in the self-assessment of their achievements and encouraging them in the development of their abilities.

To have positive self-esteem children need self-confidence and this can be powerfully developed when children are encouraged to use their initiative, to make decisions and to be responsible for sharing in the planning and the evaluation of their work. If we want children to develop positive self-esteem, then we have to show them that they are capable, however young they are, of decisions which have an impact on their own experiences and their own lives. Children who are proud of their cultural heritage, their gender, their family and themselves have been profoundly affected by the attitudes of those around them and the teacher is a critical part of that network of influence. If we are to make observations of children which are reflective of the best that they can do, and in which they have the confidence to share with us what they know, then we must provide them with an environment which encourages their confidence and builds their self-esteem.

A range of peers

As early years practitioners, we are rightly concerned with the social development of children. As with all other aspects of their development, the social experiences of children before they start at school will vary enormously. Some may have come from large, extended family groups which include brothers, sisters, uncles, aunts and grandparents. Some may have had significant periods of time with child minders or at playgroup or nursery and have become used to working and playing alongside their peers. But, for some children, school will be their first introduction to the competition, collaboration and cooperation that is required when you are one among a number of others, all vying for space, resources and attention. Like all skills, being sociable is something you get better at with practice. The more people you meet, the more you learn to adjust and adapt to differences in attitudes and behaviour. Some people are better at this than others; some children are better at this than others. Home circumstances, life experiences and general dispositions will mean that certain children are ready to work in a range of social situations while others need support to increase their social skills. The more opportunities children have to work alongside the full range of children in the class, the more opportunities they will have to learn those social skills which will make school life, and life in general, a more positive and pleasurable experience. If young children are grouped early, in fixed groups, they may miss out on many of these valuable social experiences (see Chapter 6). Children should be able to communicate and cooperate with a range of others irrespective of their gender, race, physical attributes or ability. A profile of the social development of the child is best founded on observations of children working alongside a range of peers, demonstrating a whole range of characteristics, attitudes and personalities.

Children working with an adult

There will be many opportunities for teachers and other adults to observe children while they are working alongside them. By supporting a child in a task, or facilitating their activity, the adult is able to observe and, if appropriate, to record what the child says and what the child does as evidence of their growing conceptual awareness or skill development. They can also observe *how* the child approaches tasks, what strategies they use for solving problems, their persistence and motivation and their attitudes in general. What has to be remembered is that the presence of the adult will, to a lesser or greater degree, alter the behaviour of the child; to what extent depends on the task and also on the sensitivity of the adult. If a child is engaged in an adult-initiated activity and that adult is close by, then the child may frequently look to the adult for affirmation that they are doing the task 'correctly'. Some recent research in a reception class (Fisher 1996) illustrates the impact of the task on children's reliance on the teacher (see Example 3).

When a teacher gives a child a task and then sits with them while they tackle it, then the child's approach and the amount of support they look for will have a significant impact on the process and probably the outcome of the task. This is not to say that a teacher

---

Example 3: Building independence

As a researcher, I spent one day a week for 2 years in the same reception class, observing the interactions throughout the day between the teacher and members of her class. There was very clear evidence that the more directed the task, the more frequently the children went to the teacher for help and, particularly, affirmation. As the teacher's aim was to make the children more independent and to give herself more time to focus on her planned activities, this observation presented her with an instant strategy for achieving both aims at once. If she wanted to be interrupted less often, and have time to work with particular children or to undertake observation, then the rest of the class had to be engaged in tasks which were less prescriptive and over which they had more control. The teacher changed the balance of the activities she planned. The activities where there was an adult present were more directed and the activities where children were working independently were more open-ended. Once this new way of planning was established, the teacher reported far less interruptions by children engaged in independent activities.

---

should not work alongside a child – far from it. The teacher's role in questioning, challenging and guiding children's learning is critical (see Chapters 1 and 4), but it is important to be sensitive to the impact the presence of a teacher, or any adult, can have on the process and outcome of any activity.

Children working independently

When children work independently, they display different behaviours and often different strategies and skills than when they work under the direction of an adult. Dependent upon how much independence they are used to in their classroom generally, observations of children working alone usually reveal fresh perspectives on the children as learners. Children's responses will be affected by whether the task is self-chosen or initiated by the teacher, whether they have been told to collaborate or whether they have chosen to do so, and whether or not there is a required end-product. Whatever the task, the conversations of children working independently usually reveal far more about children as learners than is revealed when they work on tasks where adults are present.

Different times of the day

Until relatively recently, it was common practice in many infant classes for children to work in the morning and play in the afternoon. Apart from the fact that this is pedagogically flawed (see Chapter 3), it also works against all that is known about human physiology. Children are no different from adults; some are 'larks' and some are 'owls' – those who wake up bright and perky and irritatingly cheerful straight away, and those who begin sluggishly, but improve as the day goes on. Observation of children at different times in the day shows us that some children take a long time to settle in the morning, whereas others can concentrate almost immediately. Some children are adversely affected by breaks in the school day (assembly, television, etc.), whereas others seem to take these in their stride. Many children are affected by playtimes and lunchtimes and take a long time to settle afterwards. My reception class research showed that it is the period from break to lunchtime which is the most disrupted. After lunchtime, children were tired but usually more able to settle to their various tasks than after break, when they were still wound up from rushing around and needed more intervention from adults to engage in their activities (Fisher 1996). Because children are human, they will be at their best at different times in the day, so it is important that when we observe them we take this into account, and do not always observe them at the same time of day, and do not always assume that all children will be at their best at nine in the morning.

The purpose of observations and conversations

Teachers who want to find out about children choose strategies which tell them most. Unless those strategies leave room for the teacher to learn from the process, then the strategies will not be informative but merely affirmative. Teachers come to know what they already know and teaching remains rooted in *assumptions* about what children need to know next.

Having made an observation or recorded important elements of a conversation, the teacher needs to translate these records into appropriate action. The professional skill of the teacher is in knowing what it is that they have seen or heard in relation to each child's development. They have to make decisions about whether what they have seen or heard means that something particular needs to be planned and whether the individual child has needs that have not previously been identified. Much of what has already been planned will remain relevant, but ongoing assessments of children inform the 'fine-tuning' of short-term plans (see Chapter 3) and enable teachers to ensure that time is spent developing a curriculum which starts from the needs and interests of the child.

Conclusion

Having conversations with children and observing them in action acknowledges the competences with which children come to school, not only at the beginning but throughout their school careers. Observations and conversations are tools for assessment which recognize children's individual competences as the baseline against which their future learning needs should be identified. Such assessment practices define the role of the teacher as being that of a learner, alongside her class, finding out about and then building on what children already know and can do. The assessment practices described in this chapter are the starting point for planning rather than the finishing point. The next chapter explores how teachers use the information gained through initial assessments of children to plan an appropriate curriculum.

3

PLANNING FOR LEARNING

Decisions about an appropriate curriculum

Introduction

Acknowledging the child as a competent learner should ensure that the starting point for planning an appropriate curriculum is the child's developing skills and understandings. These competences are established through the initial assessments of children described in the previous chapter. What children already know and can do should determine the experiences which are planned for their development (Bruce 1987; DES 1990; EYCG 1992; Ball 1994). However, the imposition of an externally imposed National Curriculum has challenged the plausibility of such a notion and many practitioners feel torn between their early years principles, rooted in the ideals of child-centredness, and their statutory obligations to meet an agenda purporting to meet the needs of all children rather than the individual learner.

The notion of child-centredness

Early childhood education is grounded in the belief that every child should receive an education designed to meet their own individual needs. Child-centred thinking has its roots in the work of philosophers such as Rousseau and Dewey and stemmed, as described by John Darling (1994) in his review of child-centred education, 'from radical dissatisfaction with traditional practice'. This practice was characterized by an emphasis on content over process and on memorizing of facts rather than an understanding of concepts. Classes were taught as a single entity, with little or no account taken of individual differences in previous experiences, current understandings or rates of progress.

The time-honoured metaphor that children were 'empty vessels to be filled' made the classroom roles of children and teachers very explicit. It was the duty of teachers to fill the vessels with knowledge and the duty of children to learn what was being taught, and if they did not, then the onus of blame was well and truly on *their* shoulders.

Yet long before such practice was established, there was a commitment to the notion of children as individual learners. As early as 1762, Jean-Jacques Rousseau in *Emile* declared that 'Nature provides for the child's growth in her own fashion, and this should never be thwarted'. His approach to thinking about children and their development was taken forward by such writers as Pestalozzi, Froebel and Dewey, each developing and revising the work of the others until a powerful philosophy for the education of young children was formed. However, it was not until the 1960s that this philosophy really began to have an impact on practice in Britain. The main reason for the change in pedagogy was the public endorsement of a more child-friendly approach by official reports, most notably *Children and their Primary Schools* (The Plowden Report) (CACE 1967). The Plowden Report heralded a more liberal view of education, encapsulated in the celebrated quotation: 'at the heart of the education process lies the child. No advances in policy, no acquisitions of new equipment have their desired effect unless they are in harmony with the nature of the child, unless they are fundamentally acceptable to him' (CACE 1967: para. 9).

Child-centred education is concerned with the *development* of children. Development is seen as a natural progression which is best aided by adults who 'have an appreciation of and respect for the ways of children' (Darling 1994: 3). This is an important element. Part of the criticism of child-centred practices was that children were able to choose and control their own actions and that the role of the teacher diminished for fear of being accused of 'interfering' with this natural development (see Blenkin and Kelly 1987; Darling 1994).

Interestingly, it was the work of Jean Piaget (1896–1980) that did much to fuel this misconception. Piaget believed that children pass through certain stages of development and cannot operate at the later stages before passing, in their own good time, through the earlier ones. This supposed that children pass through these stages irrespective of adult support and that the best that an adult can do is to interfere! The obvious assumption was that if children passed naturally through these stages of development, then the most dangerous thing one could do was to rush them through the process. This led to the notion of 'readiness' (see Chapter 1), with teachers believing that they had to *wait* until a child was ready to learn something, rather than being in a position to move them on or extend them beyond the stage they were at. Such a notion rendered the teacher somewhat impotent. Knowing the next stage of development and perceiving the learning needs of the child are of restricted use if one believes that it is damaging to use such knowledge. Another facet of Piaget's work which apparently diminished the role of the teacher was his emphasis on the child as an individual explorer of the world, discovering and making sense of new situations through action and self-directed problem solving (Bruner and Haste 1987). Piaget's influence on thinking and practice in the 1960s and 1970s caused many practitioners, as well as critics, to believe that the role of the teacher had been sidelined and that children were to be encouraged to do as they please. The power of these assumptions can be seen all too clearly in the series of *Black Papers* written between 1969 and 1977 (see Cox and Dyson 1969a, 1969b, 1970; Cox and Boyson 1975, 1977) and the impact of the resultant conservative backlash is still being felt today.

Much of Piaget's work became challenged even by those who acknowledge his tremendous contribution to the development of our thinking about children and their learning. One of the most influential challenges came from his colleague Margaret Donaldson. In *Children's Minds*, Donaldson (1978) argued for a fresh interpretation of Piaget's views based on her own research in which she replicated some of Piaget's tests but using significantly different methodology. She and her colleagues found that by setting Piaget's tasks in contexts which were familiar to the children and using language which was clear and relevant to the tasks, significantly more children were able to complete the tasks than had succeeded in Piaget's original tests (Piaget and Inhelder 1956). Donaldson's work adds powerful weight to the notion of the young child as a competent learner and the critical role of the teacher in extending those competences:

the normal child comes to school with well-established skills as a thinker. But his thinking is directed outwards on to the real, meaningful, shifting, distracting world. What is going to be required for success in our educational system is that he should learn to turn language and thought in upon themselves. He must be able to direct his own thought processes in a thoughtful manner. He must become able not just to talk but to choose what he will say, not just to interpret but to weigh interpretations. His conceptual system must expand in the direction of increasing ability to represent itself. He must become capable of manipulating symbols.
(Donaldson 1978: 88–9)

As was described in Chapter 1, Lev Vygotsky (1896–1934) offered a very different view of the role of the teacher. Vygotsky saw children's cognitive development operating at two levels, the present level and the potential level. He believed that the role of more knowledgeable others is to move the child from the actual to the potential next level of understanding. The task of the teacher is to encourage children to do *without* help what they can do only at present *with* help (Anning 1991). In other words, children's learning can be extended by the right intervention at the right time.

> Teachers have a highly interactive role in a Vygotskian frame-work. Children's development is static unless they are able to work in their zone of proximal development. Teaching does not wait upon development but propels it.
>
> (Smith 1993: 56)

This support for children's learning is what Wood *et al.* (1976) have called 'scaffolding', and this offers an appropriate metaphor for the notion of child-centredness in its aim to plan activities, resources and interactions which match the level of competence and maturity of the child. The work of Jerome Bruner is of particular relevance to early years practitioners because he works from an analysis of children's learning, to a model of classroom pedagogy and then to a curriculum framework. It is the very fact that the National Curriculum works in precisely the opposite way that seems to set it at odds with the notion of child-centredness.

Comparisons between the pioneers and modern theorists

The child-centred notions of Rousseau, Dewey, Pestalozzi and others can be seen clearly in the principles and practice of the early child-hood educators such as Froebel, Montessori and Steiner. Tina Bruce's (1987) book, *Early Childhood Education,* takes the threads of influence even further by comparing the principles of those early pioneers with the work of more modern theorists such as Piaget, Vygotsky, Bruner and Mia Kelmer Pringle, founding Director of the UK National Children's Bureau. The 'Ten Common Principles of the Pioneers' (Bruce 1987) are a valuable framework for the development of good early years practice in current settings.These principles have been adopted and developed in many subsequent documents (e.g. EYCG 1992; Roberts 1995b). The Oxfordshire Early Years Team (1996) have adapted them to reflect their work with children aged 0–8 years, and this adaptation offers indicators of those early years principles in practice.

Principles of early childhood education

1 *Childhood is seen as valid in itself. It is a stage of life and not simply a preparation for the future.*

- Experiences and environment should be appropriate to the age and developmental stage of the child.
- Experiences should be relevant to the child's *current* needs.
- Each child should be valued for themselves, what they are, what they know and what they can do.
- Learning at this stage may improve later performance but, first and foremost, learning enables children to achieve their present potential and enriches and fulfils their present life (Moss and Penn, 1996).

2 *The whole child is considered to be important; social, physical, intellectual, moral and spiritual aspects of development are related.*

- All aspects of the child should be considered in planning provision and experiences.
- The balance between these areas needs to be sustained once children begin statutory schooling.
- All areas of development should be observed and assessed in order to inform future planning.

3 *There is potential in all children which will emerge powerfully under favourable conditions. Each child is unique and special, with individual ways of learning.*

- Every child should be known well by at least one adult.
- Children should be valued with full regard to their gender, race and ability.
- The environment should be sufficiently flexible and responsive to meet the range of children's learning styles and strategies.
- Children need time and space to produce work of quality and depth (EYCG 1992).

4 *Parents are the first and continuing educators of their children. Schools should value and build on parental expertise.*

- Schools need to establish systems where parents can tell the school about their child.

- Schools should develop a partnership with parents and carers based on mutual respect and a shared interest in the child.
- Parents should be involved in the process of assessment and contribute to decisions about future plans for their child.

5 *Learning is holistic and interconnected. The young child does not separate experiences into different compartments.*

- Short-term planning should be sufficiently flexible to make space/allow time for the children's spontaneous interests.
- Planning should identify the understanding, skills and attitudes which are important for developing learners; activities and topics should support rather than determine these objectives.
- Broadly based and integrated experiences are appropriate when working within the National Curriculum.

6 *Young children learn through exploration, play and talk.*

- Young children learn most effectively by doing rather than being told (EYCG 1992).
- Play should occur throughout the day, alongside teacher-directed activity.
- Play is given status when it is valued, assessed and used to extend learning.
- Children should be encouraged to initiate conversations and pose questions.

7 *Our starting points for supporting learning are what children* can do *and what they* can nearly do.

- Children should be helped to identify their own targets and achievements.
- Observation-based assessment should be the basis for planning.
- Adults should sensitively support and extend children's learning.

8 *Intrinsic motivation is recognized and valued as a powerful force for learning.*

- Autonomy (physical, social and intellectual) and self-discipline are emphasized.

- Children should have periods of time for sustained self-initiated activity.
- Children should have the opportunity to make choices and decisions.

9 *The relationships which children establish with adults and other children are of central importance in their development.*

- The education of young children should be the responsibility of appropriately trained and experienced educators with a knowledge of child development.
- Children need planned experiences which encourage the interpersonal and cognitive skills necessary for collaboration and cooperation.
- Teachers should be aware of themselves as models.

10 *Children's education is seen as the total experience of, and interaction with, their environment.*

- Children's schooling should draw on their personal context of family, culture and community.
- There should be provision and planning for an indoor and outdoor environment of equal quality.
- The way in which we talk and respond to children throughout their time in school should create a climate which nurtures self-esteem.

The translation of principles into practice has been influenced in particular by the writing of Geva Blenkin, who espouses a commitment to a developmental view of education and argues cogently for a concept of education:

not as a device for the transmission of certain bodies of agreed knowledge and values or as a process of moulding people into some predetermined shape, it is of the enhancement of capacities, the widening of every person's horizons of appreciation and understanding, the maximization of everyone's potential, the development of everyone's powers of self-direction, autonomy, understanding and critical awareness.

(Blenkin and Kelly 1987: 11)

In Chapter 2 of *The National Curriculum and Early Learning*, Blenkin (1994) draws together four broad themes of early childhood education which, based on the principles of a developmental curriculum, are peculiar to that stage of education:

1 The young child is dependent on adults and is new to institutional life. The process of learning to be a pupil is thus of great importance.
2 Rates of development and learning are at their most rapid during this stage of education, and they are highly susceptible to environmental constraints and advantages. The young child, therefore, needs to be stimulated by a wide range of experiences rather than confined to a narrow and restrictive programme.
3 Although social interaction is important at every stage of learning, it is of particular importance at this early stage, since young learners are not able to make sense of experiences which are repesented in a more formal or abstract way.
4 Early education must not only provide a rich array of practical experiences, but it must also nurture the playfulness of children. For secure mastery of skills or knowledge depends on play, because it is through play that the child is able to test out, informally and personally, what is newly learnt.

As early years practitioners, we are challenged to plan a curriculum which:

• focuses on process rather than content or outcome (or attainment targets?);
• offers a wide range of experiences rather than a restrictive one (or imposed one?);
• emphasizes first hand, real experiences which contextualize learning (rather than a diet of workbooks or worksheets?); and
• emphasizes active learning and play (rather than pencil and paper recording?).

It would seem that the fundamental tenets of good early years practice fly in the face of a National Curriculum which is designed and imposed without any knowledge of, or seeming concern for, the individual child, and fails to recognize 'what a complex and subtle matter is the learning of pupils in their early, formative years' (Blenkin and Kelly 1994: 197).

The National Curriculum and early learning

Blenkin and Kelly's critique of the National Curriculum outlines certain key features which they believe renders it wholly inappropriate as a curriculum framework for young children. First it does not take account of the intellectual needs of young children or see them as being qualitatively different from those of older pupils. Second, it ignores the 'manifest advantages of play' and the merits of a holistic approach to the curriculum. Third, it does not acknowledge that young children need assistance to structure their own knowledge and make sense of their own worlds. Fourth, it takes a limited and simplistic view of what the teaching and learning of subjects entails in the early years. Fifth, it has no research base of its own and manifestly ignores the accumulating research evidence for appropriate high-quality early years education (see Sylva 1994). Finally, what is happening in England and Wales is in 'stark contrast' to policy developments in almost every other country in the world.

The realities of the impact of the National Curriculum highlight some interesting features, many of which correlate with the views of Blenkin and Kelly. One study of school and classroom practice in a local authority in Wales (Cox and Sanders 1994) revealed that irrespective of the status given to play in the documentation, the National Curriculum had reduced 'the scope for Year 1 teachers to engage in their children's free play activities'. Some headteachers expressed concern about the premature introduction of very young children to the more formal National Curriculum, which supports the developmental principle that the curriculum should not be formalized too early as this is likely to alienate young learners (EYCG 1995). A particularly worrying feature of this research was the number of teachers who reported that the introduction of the National Curriculum had put greater pressure on slower learning children in order to reach the appropriate attainment targets, with a consequent damaging effect on their motivation and self-esteem.

Both headteachers and class teachers perceived a change in the status and nature of the topic or cross-curricular approach to teaching, with the choice of topics apparently constrained by the recent emphasis upon whole-school planning. There was an interesting dichotomy in that some class teachers expressed the view that a cross-curricular approach to the teaching of the National Curriculum was the only way to cover its breadth, while others thought that it would be impossible to cover the National Curriculum in this way. Given the early childhood principle about not compartmentalizing learning (Bruce 1987), there was alarming evidence of a number of head-teachers, not perhaps early years specialists themselves, who believed that discrete subject teaching would increasingly have a place in the teaching of the National Curriculum – and these were headteachers of schools with Key Stage 1 children (5–7 years).

The research of Cox and Sanders underlines evidence collected from larger, national studies (e.g. the PACE study, Osborn and Pollard

1991; the Leverhulme study, Bennett *et al.*1992) and their findings are backed up in the reported observations of Her Majesty's Inspectorate (HMI) and the Office for Standards in Education (Ofsted), all acknowledging that particular concern has been expressed about the standardized, formal assessment of young children's attainments. This clearly runs counter to the developmental approach, encouraging diagnostic assessment of individual children 'based on teachers' observations and recordings of each child's special interests and developmental progress' (Bradekamp 1987: 3).

Two findings of the PACE Project ('Primary Assessment Curriculum and Experience', centred at the Universities of Bristol and the West of England) are of particular relevance to early years practitioners. The first of these is that the proportion of class teachers who felt they had less freedom in their choice of teaching methods than previously increased between 1990 and 1992. The second is that teachers' ability to respond to topics introduced by children and to create activities around them was being eroded, surely one of the most vital elements of successful early years practice. Both of these issues are addressed later in this book.

Subject knowledge

Contrary to their avowed aim not to dictate *how* teachers should go about the business of teaching, the Department for Education (DFE) commissioned a 'discussion document' entitled *Curriculum Organisation and Classroom Practice in Primary Schools: a discussion paper* (Alexander *et al.* 1992), which was intended to stimulate debate about a whole variety of aspects of classroom practice which were largely concerned with how teachers go about the business of teaching. The document created more than mere debate over a series of issues, but the issue of subject knowledge and the deployment of subject specialists in primary schools is one which has had a profound effect already, not only on existing early years practitioners, but on those who are being trained to work in the early years. The problem of shortage of subject expertise in primary schools was described as 'acute' and the report advocated that every primary school should have direct access to specialist expertise in all nine national curriculum subjects and in religious education. This has not only led to an increase in single subject teaching, but also to the reintroduction in some schools of the practice of streaming with its inherent discrimination against pupils' actual abilities and needs. These practices have been adopted in infant schools as well as junior schools even though they cut across the principles of an integrated curriculum. It is important to remember that the discussion document was not specifically aimed at Key Stage 1 children, but intended for debate about 'the successful implementation of the National Curriculum particularly at *Key Stage 2*' (Alexander *et al.* 1992: para. 1, emphasis added). However, as so often happens, the early years and Key Stage 1 were brought together in the discussion document with Key Stage 2 under the banner of 'primary' schooling and headteachers and practitioners who were not sufficiently knowledgeable or committed to appropriate early years practice adopted the 'writing on the wall' with an alacrity which has been positively alarming. While it is inevitable that teachers of younger children feel a downwards pressure from the implementation of changes further along the educational path, it is equally important to resist such pressures when they would bring about practice that is inappropriate for young learners. In particular, those responsible for managing the education of children in the early years should be sufficiently knowledgeable about the learning needs of young children to make decisions about policy and practice which are rooted in the principles of early childhood education.

The pressure to reaffirm subject expertise has had an immediate impact on initial teacher education, and courses for students wishing to teach in the early years have been affected by two issues. First, it has been deemed desirable that 'primary teachers' (the collective grouping again) should have knowledge of subject application for Key Stage 2 children as well as early years and Key Stage 1, irrespective of whether or not students have any intention of teaching this age group. Thus the time that can be devoted to the highly complex and demanding job of being an early childhood specialist has been reduced dramatically. Second, the government bodies which control the content of courses for institutions of higher education have emphasized such high percentages of subject knowledge and application that it has squeezed out the non-statutory element of child development, knowledge of which is still at the heart of all successful early years practice. Teachers of young children need to know how children develop just as much, if not more, than how subjects develop. The Rumbold Report, *Starting with Quality* (DES 1990), stated unequivocally that 'For the early years educator ... the process of education – *how* children are encouraged to learn – is as important as, and inseparable from, the content – *what* they learn' (para. 68). It is a lack of understanding of young children's learning processes and the impact these have on their educational development which characterizes current policy decisions. If children's learning were uniform and their responses mechanical, then a curriculum which focused on 'delivery' would not only be appropriate but effective. But it is the idiosyncratic nature of learning which makes teaching so demanding and, of course, so rewarding. How dull it would be if all children learned in the same way, with the same motivation, at the same rate and with the same result. But if we begin to train generations of teachers who do not know what to do when children respond in unexpected ways, then the blame will revert to the children. Teachers need to look reflectively at their own practice and make adaptations and adjustments in order to teach all children effectively.

There is little disagreement among educationalists that an essential aspect of teaching is an understanding of the major disciplines and the means for making these accessible to young children (Aubrey 1994). But the world of school has been shown by Donaldson (1978) and Tizard and Hughes (1984) to be discontinuous with the rest of the child's world. The *application* of subject knowledge and expertise is most successful when students and teachers learn about how children learn and develop, so they can apply the subject in contextually appropriate ways and the generalized mass of subject matter can be taught effectively to a range of children with a range of learning needs. Calderhead and Miller (1985) suggest that teachers interweave knowledge of subjects with a knowledge of classroom realities to create 'action-relevant' knowledge – the kind of knowledge that you *really* need when faced with a class of interested and lively 5-, 6- or 7-year-olds.

Although every child (and indeed every adult) brings a unique set of experiences and understandings to each learning situation, it is possible – and, as far as the teacher is concerned, essential – to see that there are also generalizable patterns in children's development. Unless teachers of young children acknowledge and articulate these patterns, they will be faced with an insurmountable task in planning and implementing a curriculum which fosters learning in a class of up to forty children. As Angela Anning (1991) stresses, it is important to retain insights into the particularities of each child as a learner and to respect their individuality, but it is equally important to acknowledge their similarities.

Similarities and differences between young learners

When considering similarities and differences, I believe that it is helpful to reflect on the need for different approaches between teaching and assessment. When making assessments, children *must* be seen as individuals. The teacher must look for what the individual knows, understands and can do. But having made these assessments, which are concerned with the individual, it will be seen that some children have similar needs as well as some having different ones. Teaching can thus be planned to meet either the similarities or the differences. On many occasions a group or class can be taught something in the same way at the same time. However, there will be some children for whom a certain stage, approach or concept is wholly inappropriate and in order to meet their particular needs something different has to be planned.

While I do believe that there are serious tensions between the National Curriculum and a developmentally appropriate early years curriculum (see Blenkin and Kelly 1987), I also believe that there are ways of looking at the apparent dichotomies which may make the application of one not wholly incompatible with the constraints of the other. I believe that the answer to the tension lies within a better definition of the major stages of curriculum planning. Schools and teachers have been increasingly required to plan in depth at each stage – long, medium and short term. Definitions of these stages have been prolific and sometimes conflicting. While not wishing to add to the plethora of definitions, I would suggest that long-term and medium-term planning meet one set of needs and short-term planning meets a different set. Long-term and medium-term planning are, in my view, about the curriculum and about subjects; short-term planning is about individual children. If we can make and sustain this differential, then it is possible to sustain a developmental position while meeting the requirements of the external agenda.

Stages of planning

Long-term planning is concerned with children's entitlement to a *broad and balanced* curriculum. It is achieved through the appropriate allocation of time to the teaching and assessment of the National Curriculum, religious education and other curriculum aspects identified by the school.

Medium-term planning addresses *continuity* and *progression* from one stage in each subject to the next, and from one class or school to the next. From the strands of subject progression, medium-term plans identify the concepts, skills, knowledge and attitudes to which children will be introduced in either 'continuing' or 'blocked' units (see SCAA 1995) over a given period of time. At this stage, the curriculum may be most effectively organized by linking different subject strands or areas of learning together.

Short-term planning is concerned with *differentiation* and planning for the needs of specific classes and individual children. It provides the detail of activities, experiences, resources, groupings and teaching strategies which are identified through ongoing observation and assessment of children in action.

Long-term planning

Long-term planning usually takes place well before the start of the new school year. In many schools, this stage of planning is formalized in planning cycles which identify the precise areas of learning to be addressed by each class, every term. Such planning, while it may conribute to overall school effectiveness (Ofsted 1994a), cannot purport to be concerned with the developmental needs of individual children because teachers have frequently not yet met their class; indeed, some children will not yet have started school! Even if the classes are known, the children's needs will have developed way beyond any planning that can be identified for them some 12 or more months prior to the teaching. Some practitioners will already be wanting to argue that a developmental curriculum should not seek to constrain the learning of a young child by even suggesting, this far in advance, what they will experience. Perhaps this is where the compromise comes in. While a curriculum is in place to which all teachers must adhere, there seems little point in offering solutions which are immediately unworkable. Long-term planning is about children's entitlement to the curriculum and most practitioners will be comfortable with a framework which is chiefly concerned with the breadth and balance of children's experiences.

Medium-term planning

It is at the medium-term planning stage that I feel most difficulties lie. Medium-term plans are usually written at the start of a new term or half-term. Although the children may now be known to the class teacher, their developmental needs are not. Children's needs change rapidly at this stage in their development – too rapidly to be predicted, with accuracy, several weeks in advance. So it is important that medium-term planning also addresses subjects rather than children. The most important feature of medium-term planning is that it should identify the concepts, skills, knowledge and attitudes which are the intended learning outcomes for that period of work. It may also show how these are to be integrated and linked together into themes or topics. However, all too often, on carefully produced planning sheets, there is a column for the activity or task which will be the vehicle for the intended learning outcomes. If a decision is made that this activity or that task will be appropriate for a child before their actual needs are known, then the decision may be the wrong one. There is a lot of sense in 'pencilling in' possible activities and accumulating a bank of ideas from which to draw, but activities are only the vehicles for learning, and planning must be sufficiently flexible to change activities and to accommodate the needs and interests of individual children, once they are known.

Topic work
Topic work acknowledges the fact that children do not naturally compartmentalize their learning into subject areas. It seeks to capitalize on the notion of cross-curricular learning, with its implications of mirroring the real-life learning of children in a range of contexts. However, I feel there is a danger that cross-curricular learning and topic work are no longer the same thing. Cross-curricular learning emphasizes the opportunities for children to cross the boundaries between traditional subjects and see the application of skills and the consolidation of concepts in experiences and activities which enable such cross-fertilization to occur. Topic work, while rooted in this notion, has been hijacked by teachers and their agenda. Increasingly as topics become planned by whole staffs together, the links that are made between areas of learning are not seen by children but engineered by teachers. They sometimes involve excruciating contortions to involve all areas of learning and the links are at times quite incomprehensible even to a trained adult who knows the game that is being played. Teachers need to guard against making topics as incomprehensible to children as subject divisions are.

Short-term planning

It is at this stage that planning moves from concerns with the curriculum and subject areas to concerns for the child. It is now that teachers have the opportunity to incorporate the developmental approach to learning, by making first-hand observations of children engaged in active learning and by conversing with children about what they have experienced. Through observation of children in action, carrying out open-ended tasks which allow them to explore and investigate, teachers can gain information about children's knowledge and understanding as well as their skills and strategies. All of this information is necessary if teachers are to plan a curriculum which has relevance and purpose for each child. The intention or objectives of the activity will come from the medium-term plans, but the actual activity, task or experience will be planned in the light of what the child already knows and can do, and what the teacher judges he or she needs to know or do next.

Assessment activities
It is at this stage that it is helpful to look again at the cycle of assessment, teaching and learning which determines the activities which teachers plan for children. As we saw in Chapter 2, assessment

activities are often seen as a check against the effectiveness of teaching, a measure of whether children have learnt what it was intended that they should learn. As such, assessment frequently comes at the end of the process and often gets tagged on to the seemingly more important stages of planning and teaching. But assessment is only ever seen as completing the cycle, then its use in informing future planning becomes very restricted. It leaves teachers either predicting or guessing what knowledge or understanding children bring to the introduction of a new concept or the learning of a new skill. Teachers often make elaborate introductions to new ideas and then use the 'discussion' time following the introduction to elicit a range of understandings from children. However, this knowledge is not always used to inform or to alter planning. If teachers always begin by teaching, then there is an implicit assumption that what has been planned is appropriate and that, apart from the need for differentiated follow-up, the needs of children will be met.

However, we have seen that children bring with them to school a whole range of knowledge, understanding and skills which are nothing to do with the formal education of school. Peers, different adults, the television, books, outings and visits all give children a vast array of insights which teachers ignore at their peril. It is inappropriate to introduce the concept of magnets to a child whose father is a scientist and who has conducted experiments with his young son since the age of 3 (see Example 4, p. 45). This is a trap that is easy to fall into but can just as easily be avoided.

A very valuable part of the planning process should be the design of activities to assess what children already know and can do (see Chapter 2). In other words, they come before the *new* skills, concepts or knowledge are introduced in order to ascertain precisely the starting points of each child's current knowledge and understanding. The tasks need to be as open-ended as possible and children should have a variety of opportunities to explore, experiment, investigate and hypothesize, giving the teacher every indication of what is currently known and understood. Such activities should encourage children to take risks so there can be no right answers and no predicted outcomes. So, for example, if a teacher's medium-term planning identifies the introduction of the concept of magnetism, the assessment activity could involve leaving on a table a variety of magnets and a variety of objects which attract or repel the magnets. The teacher can then observe from a distance how different children approach the investigation of these resources and listen to the conversations they have with each other, in order to learn what they already know and understand. Example 4 is an observation made of William, aged 4 years 10 months, in the classroom.

Example 4: What William already knew and understood

William stayed at the 'magnet' table for 12 minutes. In that time he did not pick up a single magnet. He became absorbed in the workings of an egg-whisk – one of the items which had been left for the investigation. He turned the handle this way and that, watching the blades rotate. He held the whisk upside down and sideways. He tried to engage another child in this investigation, but the boy was too busy discovering for himself that 'you can make it stick through paper ... look!'. William persevered until, having exhausted his investigations, he looked for the teacher and went over to show her what he had discovered. As a result of this, she was able to plan for him to use a construction kit that enabled him to make his own 'blades' using cogs and wheels. The child was the son of the scientist. He didn't need to explore the properties of magnets, he knew about them. By setting up this experience, the teacher not only reminded herself of William's knowledge and under-standing in this area – and, to varying levels, that of three other children in the class – but she was able to offer William something to meet his particular and highly specialized needs. As already noted, when making assessments of children, teachers will not find that every single child needs something different every single time. In this instance, William needed something highly specific. The other three children with experi-ence of magnets needed something else; and the remaining children all needed similar experiences because they were new to magnets and their properties and needed time to come to understand the concept of magnetism through further investigation and exploration.

There are many occasions when assessment should *begin* the cycle of teaching and learning and teachers' plans should remain flexible until precise knowledge of the children is gained. There is always a danger that when involved in long- and medium-term planning, teachers draw on records from previous teachers/year groups and, if an area or subject has not been covered in a previous class, then the assumption is made that an individual child knows nothing about it. All the children then receive the same starting point or complete scheme of work according to the presumed lack of knowledge. As pro-fessional educators we must make it our business to find out what indi-vidual children already know and can do and ensure that our planning builds on this knowledge.

Differentiation

While long- and medium-term plans are the concern of the staff as a whole and may well be similar in format, short-term planning should be more responsive to the requirements of individual teachers. Teachers need to adopt strategies which allow for these short-term plans to address the issue of *differentiation*. Differentiation is the key to matching work to the developmental needs of children.

Most recent reports on the quality of primary education have confirmed that the quality of learning experiences is related to the degree of match between any planned task and a child's previous experiences and current educational needs. Research into classroom practice (Galton *et al.* 1980; Bennett *et al.* 1984) and government-generated reports (Ofsted 1991, 1993a, 1994b) suggest that this match is frequently not achieved. It would appear that teachers often direct the level of their planning towards children of average ability, with the consequent underestimation of high attainers and the overestimation of low attainers.

There are undoubtedly many reasons why this situation exists at this time. First, there is an overload of curriculum content and assessment practices (Campbell *et al.* 1993) and these have to some extent been addressed by the revised National Curriculum (DFE 1995). Second, some teachers' classroom management strategies do not allow for observations to be made on which they can base effective, detailed assessments of individual children. Third, where teachers are shown to have differentiating practices, these have more frequently been related to unsubstantiated teacher expectation rather than children's educational needs (see Chapter 6 for a discussion of criteria for grouping children).

However, as differentiation is so critical to children's development and progress, it is important that teachers clarify what elements of their planning can be matched more closely to children's differing needs.

Differentiation may be concerned with:

- The **concepts, skills, knowledge and attitudes** which are the intended outcomes of an activity.
- Whether these are to be introduced/developed/consolidated (the **spiral curriculum**).
- The **activity** itself – different activities can be vehicles for the same outcomes and differ according to the interests of the children.
- The **introduction** to an activity – more or less detailed, verbal or written, etc.
- The **process** of an activity, determined by the importance of the

outcome; not necessarily uniform, but open to the most effective strategy for the child/group.

- The **outcome** of an activity, determined by the importance of the process; it may be open to interpretation by the child/group.
- The **support** given to an activity by an adult or other children, which may be minimal or substantial.
- The **resources** planned – different levels and different kinds.
- The **evidence** of learning, which varies according to the intended outcomes.
- The **collection** of evidence – which technique, by whom, when.
- The **assessment** of work – by the adult, child or both
- By whose **criteria** – adult, child or both.
- Follow-up **action** – what, for whom, how, when.

There is no need for every element of this process to be addressed on every occasion. But it is important that all of these elements are open to change and adaptation in order to make learning experiences relevant, meaningful and effective for children. Sometimes the teacher plans for differentiation before an activity takes place – that is *differentiation by input*. Sometimes the activity is planned in such a way that it is

---

Short-term plans

Intended learning outcomes

- Why are the children doing this activity? (from medium-term plans)
- What do I intend that they should learn?
- What concepts/skills/knowledge/attitudes are to be introduced/developed/consolidated?

Play/activity/experience

- What play/activity/experiences will meet the intended learning outcomes?
- Do the children all need the same play/activity/experiences?
- Do I need to differentiate the introduction/the process/the outcome?
- Who will give the support or will children work independently?
- What grouping is most appropriate?
- What resources are needed? Are they the same for all children?
- Does the play/activity/experience meet the learning requirements of children with special needs?

Assessment

- What evidence do I need to gather?
- Will this enable me to assess the intended learning outcomes of the play/activity/experience?
- Is it possible to gain my evidence through first-hand observation or through conversations with children?
- Will this be done during or after the play/activity/experience?
- If evidence is to be recorded by an adult, what vocabulary, actions, behaviours are they looking for? How will the adult record this?
- If evidence is to be recorded by children, will they be able to select their own method of recording and then explain it to an adult or their peers?
- Should samples of work be saved or photographs or tape-recordings taken?
- What method of assessment will be most appropriate for the play/activity/experience planned?
- In what way might children be involved in assessing their own work?
- Were the intended learning outcomes achieved?
- If not, why not? What do I need to change?
- If the learning was not what I expected, what *did* I learn about the children from the outcomes of the activity?

N.B. Be prepared to note unplanned and unexpected assessments too!

Action

- Do I need to review my short-term planning?
- Does a child/group/the class need to revisit a concept or have further practice of a skill?
- Should a child/the children have experience of working with a different child/children?
- Does a child/group need more support at the next stage of development?
- Does the child/group need different resources to support their learning?

appropriate for all children and the differentiation is seen in the way in which individuals respond to and learn from the activity – that is *differentiation by outcome*. A prompt sheet for supporting the planning of differentiated activities is given on pp. 47–8). Rather than offering a format for short-term planning, I think a prompt sheet is more helpful so that, irrespective of the format which suits the individual teacher, plans can be checked against certain indicators of differentiation. The list is offered as a starting point. You may find it helpful to formulate your own list with colleagues from your school.

Conclusion

This chapter has been concerned with planning a curriculum which acknowledges the developmental needs of children within the constraints of an externally imposed framework. It has been suggested that this is most easily done when long-term and medium-term planning are seen as meeting the development of the curriculum and short-term planning is seen as meeting the development of the child. An early years curriculum is concerned with process before product and, fortunately, at Key Stage 1, so largely is the National Curriculum. If experiences are planned which meet the principles of developmentally appropriate practice, then teachers generally find that much of the national curriculum programmes of study are also addressed. An appropriate curriculum is one that meets the needs and interests of children and also introduces children to a range of skills and concepts which are deemed by adults to be relevant and desirable for their education. The task of the teacher is to fuse together these dual interests and to ensure that the balance of children's experiences do not lead them to believe that education is something that is imposed by somebody else. Education should be a dynamic and liberating experience. If children are to be life-long learners, then the seeds for their independence and self-motivation to learn must be sown in the earliest days of their school experience. The next chapter examines how teachers achieve a balance in classroom activities and explores the role that teachers adopt in supporting the development of competent young learners.

4

THE ROLE OF THE TEACHER

Making the best use of teaching time

Introduction

The role of the teacher is inextricably bound up with how children are viewed as learners. As has already been shown, once it is acknowledged that children are competent (albeit inexperienced) learners, then teachers must be responsive to their varied and various abilities. Whatever it is intended that children should learn and however it is intended that they should learn it, the most effective learning is rooted in previous experience (Donaldson 1978; Wood 1988; Meadows 1993). Children are active learners, constantly constructing their own internal model of the world (Wells 1986). By acknowledging this, teachers reject a 'transmission' approach to teaching, where the teacher is seen as having, or having access to, knowledge and skills which it is their responsibility to transmit to the learner. Instead, teachers adopt what Rowland (1984: 4) describes as an 'interpretive' model of teaching, which involves 'not only the child's attempt to interpret and assimilate the knowledge and skills offered by the teacher, but also the teacher's growing understandings of the world'.

If we ignore what children already know and can do, then their learning will not be embedded in what is already secure and what already makes sense to them. This sends messages to children that their competences and contributions are not valued and this in turn can have a serious impact on their self-esteem.

The teacher as observer

We saw in Chapter 2 that in order to incorporate what children already know and can do, teachers need to spend a considerable amount of time finding out what that is. Time for observation needs to be found not just at the beginning of the school year or term but throughout each teaching day, so that planning is constantly informed by observations of children in action as learners. The problem for many teachers is that sitting still, not obviously engaged in interaction with a child or group of children, seems to be almost immoral! Teachers are so used to orchestrating a myriad of different activities all at the same time and being immersed in the action, that sitting back and simply watching children at work goes against the grain. But time for observation is critical. If teachers do not watch children at work, then many important moments in their development may be missed. Of course teachers can and do make observations of children when they are working alongside them, but the nature of these observations is different. Children react and respond in different ways when teachers work alongside them, and if teachers want to see how children work independently or alongside their peers, then they need to remove themselves from the situation and not be distracted by having more than one role at a time.

Making time for observation may seem daunting. However, if time is not set aside for focused observation of children at work, then teachers will not collect sufficient information about children as learners and planning will not be rooted in strong enough evidence of what children know and can do. Teachers who spend a significant amount of their time observing children say that the knowledge they gain enables them to plan far more appropriately for the individual child, group or class the next day or week. Time is not wasted in working with a child or group on an activity which is too easy or too difficult and time is not wasted in repeating or revisiting work unnecessarily. Time is actually *saved*, because teachers are able to differentiate their planning on the basis of their increased knowledge about the children in their class.

Teachers need to make time to observe children during the teaching day. As with so many things in the classroom it is a question of prioritization, but if time spent on observation saves time in planning and teaching and makes these more effective, then it is time well spent. One successful way of making time for observation is by setting time aside at the short-term planning stage when decisions are being made about which activities the teacher is going to work with most closely – I call these *teacher-intensive* activities.

Teachers are all too aware of how short the school day is and the planning of their own time needs to be undertaken carefully. It also needs to be realistic. Teacher planning needs to create time for observation rather than it being fitted into snatched moments in the day. One way of achieving this is to identify in the teacher's daily plans (a) what/who is to be *taught* and (b) what/who is to be *observed*. In this way, the teacher can see whether, given the time available, the two sets of teacher activities can be realistically achieved. As we have seen, observation is a critical part of the teaching process. The planning of the curriculum is informed by the observations that teachers make, and such an important process takes time. Planning for observation in this deliberate way may mean that time is taken from time which was previously set aside for direct involvement with children. But observation is part of the role of the teacher; it can only be done when children are at work or play and it should be done regularly when children are working independently of the teacher. A plan detailing both the teaching and observation tasks for the day can help teachers to raise the status of classroom observation and give it the time it needs.

The teacher as 'teacher'

Making good use of time does not, of course, only apply to observation. A teacher has many roles to fulfil, but very little time in which to do it. When looking to make the best use of teaching time, it is necessary to be realistic. If the classroom situation is such that there is one teacher and possibly twenty, thirty or forty children, then the teacher has one of two choices. The easiest option is to teach the class as though it were a single unit, delivering the same curriculum to all children at the same time. This means that the class size is relatively immaterial because the onus is on the children to receive and inwardly digest the curriculum. But any teacher knows that this will not guarantee learning. The same diet of experiences can be delivered to a class of children and their digestion of those experiences will be different. Some children will go hungry, some will end up feeling sick, some will turn up their noses because they don't like what's on offer, and some will eat the bits they enjoy and leave the rest on the plate. It is the very fact that children cannot be fitted neatly into a curriculum but need a curriculum which fits *them* that makes teaching so challenging.

Teachers need to consider a different option. Although there are times when effective teaching and learning take place in a large group, for the majority of their classroom experience young children need to work (individually, in a pair or in a group) on activities which they will carry out independently. Such activities need to be sustained by individuals or groups so that they do not need to interrupt the teacher at work with her *teacher-intensive* activity. These more independent activities I call *teacher-initiated* activities. In an early years classroom, then, there are usually two main types of activity going on at any one time, which have been instigated by the teacher:

- *Teacher-intensive activities*: these are activities in which the teacher is directly and constantly engaged with children.
- *Teacher-initiated activities*: these are activities which the teacher initiates, but which the children will work on largely independently.

Teacher-intensive activities

Recent reports on classroom practice have highlighted the need for teachers to spend *focused* time with the child/children with whom they are working. For example, the HMI response (Ofsted 1993a) to the discussion paper by the 'Three Wise Men' (Alexander *et al.* 1992) identifies 'teaching targeted to specific individuals or groups' as one factor associated with better classroom practice. So, if focused time is being given to only some of the class, then the important question is, what are the rest of them doing? Planning for and working with the teacher-intensive group is not the problem. Planning for and ensuring the quality of the activities of the rest of the class is.

Teacher-initiated activities

Teachers have first to consider the activities they want to work on *with* children, and then plan for other activities which the rest of the class will be doing independently. The first step towards addressing this issue is the realization that the nature of what children do when they are working with a teacher is significantly different from the nature of an activity when children work without the teacher. Activities which children undertake independently are not simply teacher-intensive activities without the teacher being there. Teacher-initiated activities differ from teacher-intensive activities in various ways. Teacher-initiated activities need to:

- be sufficiently *clear* for children to be able to work without constantly checking that what they are doing is 'right';
- be sufficiently *motivating* that they will sustain the interest and involvement of the children so that they do not interrupt the teacher;
- involve an element of *problem-solving* so that children do not quickly come up with 'right answers';
- be sufficiently *open-ended* for children to be able to extend them in ways that interest and engage them.

The key is the open-endedness. The minute that an activity is so tightly prescribed by a teacher that there is clearly only one way of doing it – and that's the teacher's way – then children will check repeatedly that what they are doing is 'right'. If teachers want uninterrupted teaching time, then a great deal of consideration needs to be given to the activities which the children are to undertake independently.

Independent learners should not be abandoned learners. When children work independently it does not mean that the teacher will not go to them, observe them in action and have conversations with them about their activities. But this should be done when the teacher has finished working with her teacher-intensive group. The teacher then moves on to the children working on teacher-initiated and child-initiated activities in order to engage in these learning experiences in whatever way is most appropriate. Once this has been achieved, the teacher returns to her next teacher-intensive activity. In this way, teachers remain in control of the use of their time and are not at the mercy of the children, servicing their needs and responding to cries for help because the tasks which were supposed to be completed independently need too much support.

If teachers are to spend focused time with an individual or small group, then most children in early years classrooms will spend most of their time working independently. It is crucial therefore, that the activities they are engaged in are worthwhile and bring about effective learning. Many children spend far too much of their school day on teacher-initiated activities for these to be mere time-fillers. It is necessary to challenge the notion that the only worthwhile learning occurs when a teacher is there. This implies that any learning that occurs when children are working independently is of little value and this patently is not true, for we have already seen that the learning which children achieve prior to receiving any kind of formal education is very effective and usually self-driven. Children are learning all the time and only a small amount of that time is spent anywhere near a teacher!

Child-initiated activity

A third kind of activity that should take place in every early years classroom is activity initiated by the children themselves. Child-initiated activities encourage children to make their own choices and decisions about what they will do, the resources and equipment they will use, and the processes and outcomes of the experience. This is *not* the kind of activity where a teacher encourages the children to use play equipment, such as plastic construction materials, and then gives them a specific task to complete with that material. This is a perfectly valid kind of activity, but it is not child-initiated. The minute a teacher has a planned intention for an activity, and directs either the process or the outcome, then that activity becomes teacher-initiated. Child-initiated activities enable children to be in control and to decide on experiences that are meaningful for them.

Child-initiated activity is central to the acknowledgement of children as competent learners. It is through such activity that young children make sense of their world, and learn to explore, experiment and take risks (Moyles 1989). The place of play is fully explored in Chapter 7, but suffice to say in this context that child-initiated activity should be part of the fabric of the early years classroom and is critical in the balance of activities which the teacher plans.

The balance of classroom activities

In the early years classroom, there should be a balance between teacher-intensive activity, teacher-initiated activity, and child-initiated activity. I find it helpful to see these three types of activity at the three corners of a triangle. The differences between the three activities can be summarized as follows:

- *Child-initiated* activities enable children to investigate and engage in tasks that have meaning and purpose for them.
- *Teacher-initiated* activities arise from the teacher's planning (i.e. an investigation of magnets) but are sufficiently open-ended for children to respond independently in a variety of ways.
- *Teacher-intensive* activities arise from the teacher's planning, but are more directed and are the focus of teacher time.

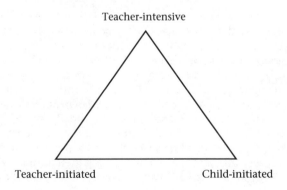

How the balance is maintained between these three types of activity will rest with the teacher and will change from day to day and sometimes session to session. But looking at classroom activities in this way helps to give a sense of perspective to the role of the teacher within the classroom. It helps to see what can be reasonably managed and addresses, in a positive way, what the rest of the class is doing. The movement of the teacher between these activities can be summarized as follows:

1 The teacher works with an individual or small group on a teacher-intensive task.
2 The rest of the class are engaged on either teacher-initiated or child-initiated activities.
3 These activities must enable children to be independent of the teacher so they do not need to interrupt the teacher-intensive task.
4 The teacher completes the teacher-intensive task and moves to both the teacher-initiated and child-initiated activities in order to support and extend these experiences as appropriate.
5 Independent learning should not be abandoned learning. Teacher involvement in all classroom activities is crucial if they are to have status and purpose.
6 Once children working independently have been adequately supported the teacher returns to the next teacher-intensive activity.
7 The rest of the class move independently between teacher-initiated and class-initiated activities until/unless the teacher draws them to a teacher-intensive task. (How children move from one activity to the next is the subject of Chapter 9.)
8 *All* classroom activities are shared at a review time during the day (see Chapter 9).

Use of teacher time

Looking at the balance between teacher-intensive, teacher-initiated and child-initiated learning gives each teacher action a clear purpose. Each role is planned, is deliberate and, most of all, it acknowledges that a classroom with one teacher and thirty or more children has to be planned for realistically. I am not suggesting that by using this management strategy children will *never* interrupt! Some children – for justifiable reasons – will occasionally need help or reassurance. But by planning teacher-initiated activities with care, the number of such interruptions will be minimized. A culture of independence surfaces in the classroom, children know that they do not need to rely on the teacher at every turn and they come to enjoy their autonomy.

The recorded interactions between a teacher and her reception class

(Fisher 1996) provide fascinating data which chronicle the growing independence of children and the changes in their attitudes and behaviour towards their teacher. At the beginning of the school year, in the autumn term, the children related to their teacher in ways that revealed their dependence on her:

Do you want me to do any more?

Can I stop this now please?

As the children became more independent, they seemed to revise their concept of what 'being a pupil' meant, started to revel in their new found independence and ignored the teacher almost completely. During the spring term the teacher was often left alone for 15–25 minutes without interruption, allowing her to get on with her teacher-intensive activities. Then, towards the end of the spring term, the relationship changed once again and the children began to refer back to the teacher, but the nature of the exchanges had altered. The children were no longer seeking reassurance, but were coming to their teacher simply to share the pleasure of a discovery or an achievement or specifically to request her support:

Do you want to see the model I've made?

Child: I can't do my a's.
Teacher: Do you want me to help?
Child: Yes.

Can you help me finish the story I'm writing?

The children's perceptions of the role of the teacher had changed. Because they were given independence and a considerable degree of autonomy in the classroom, they came to see their teacher as yet another valuable resource, enabling them to complete their tasks in hand.

Differentiation

Child-initiated activities will be, by their very nature, differentiated by outcome. Children's own decisions about activities are a reflection of their ability, their knowledge, their understanding and their skill. Observation of these activities will inform the teacher of these, and of the child's attitudes and motivation. They show the child's confidence and self-esteem, their perseverance and persistence and their willingness to try new things or their need to repeat what is familiar.

Teacher-initiated activities are best planned so that differentiation will be by outcome. Sometimes it is appropriate that an activity is planned for a group of children of certain ability and that this activity is exclusively for them. But more often than not, the very nature of an open-ended, problem-solving task is that children will tackle the task at their own level. As long as there is no 'right answer' and children know that their own solution will be valued, then the same task for a range of children is, in this instance, preferable. Differentiation by outcome places an emphasis on the teacher learning *about* children through the selected activity, as much as children learning *from* the activity.

Teacher-intensive activities are most likely to be differentiated by input. In other words, the teacher has planned to work with a group of children who have reached the same stage at the same time and will benefit from being introduced to, or consolidating, or revisiting an activity, task or experience together. The teacher's knowledge of the needs of these children will have come directly from her first-hand observations of them at work independently and as they work with adults.

Independent learning

Several groups of students and school staffs with whom I have worked have found it beneficial to explore the nature of teacher-initiated activities. Working together and sharing subject expertise, groups of practitioners can brainstorm experiences/activities across all curriculum areas, which they believe to be worthwhile independent learning opportunities for children. These experiences/activities are then shared and the group debates whether and at what point children will have recourse to an adult. Some staffs have then compiled their own bank of such activities, amending and commenting on those which work particularly well or those which did not produce the independence anticipated.

Worksheets

We cannot leave the subject of independent learning without addressing the issue of worksheets. Worksheets are frequently given to children to keep them occupied while the teacher does something else. Therefore, I want to look at worksheets in the light of their role as time-fillers and examine whether they are an effective learning mechanism for young children. The following issues should be considered:

1 The difference between many children's literacy skills and their conceptual understanding is great. Some children may have a relatively sophisticated understanding of a concept and yet be unable to record this because worksheets use language which they cannot

read or do not understand, or because their own written language is not sufficiently advanced.

2 Worksheet answers can be copied or guessed. As so many worksheets simply require gaps to be filled in, the chances of doing either or both is quite high. Such worksheets may only show how able another child is on the same table.

3 Worksheets restrict what a young child can tell you about what they know and understand. If children devise their own ways of recording knowledge and understanding, then they will select ways which make sense to them and which give all the information they want to share.

4 Worksheets clone children into producing the same answers to fill in uniform gaps.

5 Children frequently spend more time colouring in worksheets than they do engaging with the concepts behind them. By the time the worksheet is finished, most young children have difficulty in recalling what it was about.

6 Young children spend far *less* time completing most worksheets than teachers spend laboriously drawing or photocopying them.

It is important, therefore, to bear the following in mind:

- If evidence of learning is needed, *watch* and *listen* to the child and record what they do and say.
- If recorded evidence is needed, let the child devise their own ways of recording.
- If time-fillers are needed, think again; address the issue of independent learning positively and initiate activities which are valuable and valid.

Motivation and perseverance

One of the greatest benefits to the teacher of encouraging independent learners is that, by and large, they also become motivated learners. This means that a teacher spends less time coercing children to complete a directed task, something which takes up both time and energy. It also means that children usually remain on task for longer and, therefore, are less likely to make demands on teacher time, which is an added bonus. Children, like adults, lack concentration when they are required to do something which they find meaningless and irrelevant. This often occurs when activities planned by teachers do not take account of the children's own experiences and interests. Not that children should only ever engage in activities they choose, but how much easier it is – for both children and adults – when children are motivated to pursue a task because they understand its purpose. Successful teachers 'go with the flow' of children, capturing and using their current interests and absorptions to plan the curriculum. If children's experiences are not embedded in their current needs and interests, then an activity can appear pointless to them and they will either rush to finish it or simply will not give it adequate attention. This is when teachers get interrupted with cries of 'I've finished', and all teachers know how aggravating that can be.

Status and quality

Some teachers are concerned that giving children too much independence will result in work of inferior quality. There are a number of ways of ensuring that this is not the case, most of which hinge on the teacher's own attitudes to the activities going on in the classroom. In order for children to value their own work, whether it is teacher-intensive, teacher-initiated or child-initiated, it has to have status. Status can be conferred by a child and their own involvement and pride in their efforts and ideas. But status is also conferred by the teacher, who confirms or denies the importance of different activities through a myriad of different messages, both explicit and implicit. All classroom activities should be worthwhile otherwise they should not be happening. Teacher-intensive, teacher-initiated and child-initiated activities should all be of value to the teacher and to the children, and should all be planned for specific learning purposes. The three kinds of activity will be given equal status if they are:

- happening at the same time as each other, not one always preceding the others because it is seen by the teacher as being more important;
- observed, monitored and assessed by the teacher when children are in action;
- the subject of conversation to find out what children have done and discovered, and to show interest in their efforts and achievements where observation has not been possible;
- used to inform future planning.

In this way, the activities in the classroom all have a clear purpose and the use of precious teaching time is maximized.

Conclusion

The role the teacher adopts in the classroom is the key to the quality of experiences planned for the child in school. If teachers are to emulate the success of children's early educators, then their role will be most successful when they facilitate and support children's learning and respond to what children initiate. But formal education has a further dimension. Teachers are responsible for transmitting the values of society and introducing children to areas of learning and experience which they might not otherwise discover for themselves. Even so, learning is most successful when the strategies which teachers use enable children to own the experiences as much as possible and to see the relevance of those experiences to their own lives.

Teachers manage a complex orchestration of activities within the classroom. As class sizes are increasing, it is imperative that teachers – and those who manage them – accept that teachers will not be directly teaching all of the children all of the time. Indeed, the reality is that more children will spend more of their school day working independently than working with a teacher. It is therefore vital for teachers to focus their attention on those activities which encourage independence and autonomy. They should be demanding and challenging and not planned in order to fill in time until the teacher is free. By looking at the balance between teacher-intensive, teacher-initiated and child-initiated activities, teachers can be both responsive to the children's needs for independence and realistic in terms of their own need to spend targeted time with individuals and groups. The next chapter explores a variety of ways of encouraging children to be independent learners and considers how the classroom can be organized to facilitate this.

5

ENCOURAGING INDEPENDENCE

The effective use of space and resources

Introduction

Teachers who spend focused time scaffolding the learning of children and making regular observations of children in action, have already created a classroom environment which encourages independence. Neither of these crucial teacher activities can be achieved satisfactorily if a teacher is constantly being interrupted with the well-worn cry 'Please miss.... what do I do next?' In order for children to be independent learners, they need a classroom environment which facilitates their independence. As far as possible, children need to manage their own resources, space and time. If children are to work independently, they need to be given systems and strategies which enable them to manage their own learning environment and sustain their own learning.

Children's early experiences

I have already suggested that to adopt effective strategies at school, we should examine more closely the learning environments in which children have spent time, prior to starting school. In these environments, children have been successful learners because:

- the world around them is an interesting place;
- young children are naturally curious;
- children want to explore, to experiment and to become competent;
- in the home and the community there are countless opportunities to do this;
- young children meet new and varied learning experiences in many contexts – the kitchen, the street, on the television, in the park;

- there is almost always an adult on hand to ask questions of and to learn from.

The classroom learning environment needs, therefore, to provide the following elements:

- new and interesting experiences;
- activities which encourage children's natural curiosity;
- opportunities to explore, experiment and become competent;
- a timetable which is sufficiently flexible to give the children some control over when and how experiences/activities/tasks are carried out;
- learning which occurs in a range of contexts – in the classroom, outside the classroom, on visits, on trips, in workplaces, in the street;
- access to adults and other expert and experienced people (including other children) who will answer and raise questions and pose challenges to extend learning and understanding.

Creating an environment for independent learners

To begin, the classroom environment must be appropriately designed in terms of space and resources.

Space

When teachers think about what they would like to have in their classrooms to stimulate and extend children's learning, they usually find that there simply is not enough space. In discussion with a group of experienced Key Stage 1 teachers about what they would *ideally* like to have in their classrooms, the following list emerged:

The indoor area

- Carpeted area(s) for (1) sharing work, (2) jigsaws, (3) games (4) construction, (5) grouping together
- Home/imaginative/role play area
- Sand tray(s) wet and/or dry
- Water tray
- Interest/discovery/exploratory area
- Bed for children to rest
- Quiet area
- Writing/mark-making area
- Reading area

- Listening area
- Music area
- Table tops
- Creative area for (1) glueing, (2) painting, (3) cutting, (4) dough, (5) clay, (6) Plasticine, (7) modelling
- Computer area.

The outdoor area

- A garden area
- Trees, bushes and seats
- Large apparatus
- An area for small apparatus (e.g. hoops, beanbags)
- An area for bikes, tricycles and trucks
- A large sand pit
- An area for water play
- An area for construction
- An area for imaginative play
- An area, in the shade, for mark-making, reading and talking.

It might be useful to draw up your own list about what you believe young children would benefit from in their learning environment at school. I suspect your list will be very similar and equally long. In doing this exercise it is important to concentrate on what children *need* and not, as yet, on the constraints of making this a reality. The chances are that there will not be enough space in any one classroom for all of these areas and experiences. So how should decisions be made about what to leave in and what to leave out?

The most important question for teachers to ask is: What do young learners need most? This should provide the foundation for all other decisions which will be made. Sometimes it is all too easy to be distracted by other issues. All the other classrooms in the school have this or that in them; the school has always been organized like X or Y; the caretaker hates clearing up sand, and so on. But at the end of the day, teachers are concerned with what is in the best interests of children and should not be swayed from using this as their yardstick. Almost inevitably, some areas will have to be left out, or at best rotated with other less important areas. However, those areas which the teacher has deemed to be invaluable will form the basis of the learning experiences of children and the decisions will have been made using the teacher's professional knowledge about the learning needs of young children.

In many early years classrooms, the majority of space is taken up by tables and chairs. Before decisions are made about prioritizing the use of the rest of the space, it is important to consider whether space given to a table and chair for every child is space well used. Bearing in mind the need for young children to engage in active learning and practical, first-hand experiences, it is worth giving some thought to the following issues:

- Tables and chairs take up a great deal of floor space.
- The removal of *one* set of tables and six to eight chairs could create space for a sand or water tray, a carpet area, an investigation/interactive area, a listening area, etc.
- Any one of these areas might be in use for *most* of the school day.
- Are tables and chairs, for every child at the same time, needed for *most* of the school day or only occasionally?
- Which use of space is most valuable for the young learner?

The same range of questions can be asked about almost all compromise situations in the use of classroom space:

- Why is this taking up space?
- Could the space be better used?
- Could this be removed?
- Who shall I get to help me?

What is eliminated should be judged less important than what remains. Teachers may need to justify their decisions to a range of people, but those decisions will be taken on more solid ground if the justification for them is that they are in the best interests of young learners.

Allocating space
Once a list of areas is established, it is helpful to plan these so that the learning environment encourages purposeful, interactive experiences. It is a good idea to experiment with possible design lay-outs on paper *before* starting to move heavy pieces of furniture around the room!

Making decisions about the use of space

- Draw up a list of those areas which are valuable for young learners.
- Prioritize them in order to make adjustments for the available space.
- Eliminate those which are of little value or seldom used.
- Plan the remaining areas within the space available.
- Be able to justify decisions on sound educational grounds.

Principles about using space

- Some areas will be determined by 'fixtures' (e.g. sinks, floor surfaces) and these need to be allocated first.
- Each area needs sufficient space for children to move around comfortably and safely.
- Some learning experiences naturally benefit from being placed alongside others (e.g. the home corner can extend to a cafe which can benefit from being near the block play area for interrelated play).
- Some areas benefit from *not* being near others (e.g. the listening area or book corner will probably be disturbed by the activity in the construction area).
- Areas are required where children can work independently, in small groups and as a large group.

Once the areas are allocated space, these can be given names and, if appropriate, labelled, so that the children are clear about what areas are appropriate for what activity. The naming and labelling gives a sense of order to what can otherwise be a very confusing environment. It might help to imagine going into an unfamiliar supermarket and looking for the washing powders or the cereals without signs which identify where these are to be found. Clearly identified classroom areas make the organization and the management of the learning environment so much more straightforward for teachers, helpers and children.

Resources

Once space has been allocated, then the resources needed in any one area should be made available. Children who are going to be independent in their learning need to know where to find resources and where to return them once they have been used.

The choice of activities should once again be determined by the needs of the young learner. If we want children to continue to explore, investigate and discover, then we should select resources and equipment which will facilitate this. Sometimes the resources which offer some of the greatest learning potential are the most expensive. Wooden blocks, for example, may seem expensive to those operating on a slim budget, but if they provide children with a wealth of experiences in aesthetics, mathematics, the processes of science and problem-solving (Gura 1992), then they offer good value for money.

Money can be wasted on resources which might preferably be replaced by *natural* resources, which take time rather than money to collect. A Sunday afternoon walk, a visit to relatives or an outing to certain shops can result in a whole host of wonderful resources for sorting, printing, selling, describing or investigating.

The first task in most classrooms is to gather together what already exists – and then be quite ruthless with anything which is out of date, inappropriate or has pieces missing. Space is at a premium in classrooms and everything that is in it should be relevant, necessary and in one piece!

It is sometimes very difficult for teachers to get rid of things, especially if they have been accumulating them 'just in case'. If there is unlimited space and these resources are not making the place look too untidy, then they can be kept. But if keeping some things means there is no space for others, or it is difficult to find or reach others, then the needs of the learners in your classroom should be prioritized. Throw out the least useful resources and those kept 'just in case'. One rule of thumb can be that if something has not been used in the course of a full academic year, it will either be thrown away or given to someone for whom it *is* appropriate and who *will* use it.

Once all unnecessary clutter has been disposed of, it is possible to identify the gaps in the available resources and decisions can be made about what needs to be added or ordered. There are many resources which can be found or scrounged rather than bought, but however resources are gathered, there are certain principles to bear in mind.

Principles about gathering resources

- Resources should be appropriate for both the girls and the boys in your class.
- Resources should encourage girls to play in areas which are traditionally the domain of boys and vice versa (i.e. clothes in the dressing-up area which will attract boys to role play).
- Resources should reflect a wide range of cultures whether they are represented by the ethnic mix in the class or not; these might include jigsaws, cooking utensils in the home corner or books.
- Resources should be appropriate for a range of special needs, interests and circumstances; no child should feel excluded from an activity or experience because the resources available reflect a cultural, gender, social or ability bias.

Having selected and gathered new resources together, these need to be sorted and allocated to the areas in the classroom in which they are most appropriate. It is particularly important that the children see the significance of this sorting process. As with many other stages of the organization of space and resources, children can be valuably involved in the process and this will be explored later. At this point, it is sufficient to suggest that adults should not make assumptions about what is 'logical' to children. There are a number of resources that can be used in more than one curriculum area and, therefore, will the allocation be made on the basis of most frequent use or most logical use? Will there be a resource area for each area of learning or is this unrealistic? It may be best to divide curriculum resources between three major areas as suggested by Janet Moyles (1992):

- *Investigation area*: essentially science, maths, technology.
- *Language area*: mainly English, history, geography.
- *Creative area*: mostly art, design, music.

There are no hard and fast rules about this. What is important however, is that the decisions which are made make sense to the children who will use them, as well as the adults, and that the classroom systems are consistently applied. In this way, resources are more likely to be found and replaced without confusion.

Once the resources have been allocated to a certain area, they can be labelled for further ease of finding and returning. Some teachers label both the resource and its location, so that even the youngest children can match an item to its correct 'home'. The labelling can be appropriate to the age and ability of the children using them. The label may be a picture which a child or adult has drawn; it may be a catalogue picture which has been cut out; it may be a word which describes the resource; it may be a coloured symbol which denotes a certain category of resource. A headteacher colleague I know and respect feels that it is better that children come to learn where things go *without* such prompts. As with all things, this is a decision for individual teachers and their children. It is also a decision, along with others to do with classroom management, which a whole staff might want to discuss. As with most aspects of an effective school, the shared discussion and decision-making within a staffroom can have a very positive impact on children's school experiences. If children are to be encouraged to be independent, then it is highly beneficial to them – and to their teachers – that there is a consistent approach throughout the school. Nothing could be more frustrating than being given independence and autonomy in one situation only to have it taken away in the next. So do raise these issues collaboratively with colleagues. If nursery children can manage the levels of independence visible in any good-quality environment, then just imagine what 7-year-olds can achieve.

In order to facilitate independence, resources need to be located in accessible places. This has implications for the amount of resources in a classroom and is the reason for suggesting that cluttered resource areas are not helpful. If resources are cluttered, muddled, piled too high or too deep, then a child or adult may not be able to see a resource let alone realize that it might be useful. They may know the resource is there, somewhere, but be unable to find it and consequently use something less helpful. Equally, they may not find a space to return it to or may feel that the space is in such a mess that they can put it anywhere, and in this way the space remains cluttered.

Resources are best placed on uncluttered surfaces, thus allowing them to be easily seen and easy to reach. This means that it is better not to have resources in cupboards with doors. Doors can hide a multitude of clutter and they also take up a lot of space. Cupboard doors have to have space in order to be opened and that space could be so much more effectively used if the doors were removed.

Finally, children and adults need to be trained to find and replace resources properly. I do not usually use the word 'train', but in this context I think it appropriate. By 'train' I mean reminded repeatedly so that it becomes habit. It will not happen by chance, neither will it happen instantly! Children need regular reminding about where resources are to be found, how to use them and where to put them back. This is particularly true if you are a reception class teacher with fresh intakes of children throughout the school year. Such strategies are best incorporated into the daily classroom routine, particularly for younger children, so that at some point in each day they watch while someone finds/replaces a certain piece of equipment or resource. This can serve two useful purposes. First, it reinforces the importance of 'a place for everything and everything in its place' and how necessary that is for a space which is being used by a lot of people. Second, it is valuable to remind children of what resources *are* available, so that they can include them in their activities as appropriate. Young children need to develop an awareness of their role in the care of the environment, not just within school but outside in the community also. They will learn the basic tenets of respect and value for the world around them if there is an ethos in the classroom which expects and encourages them to care for, and be responsible for, their own learning space.

Finally, children need to be given time at the end of sessions to be responsible for sorting and tidying their own areas and activities so that they learn to be responsible for their own learning environment and appreciate the necessity, for everyone's sake, to keep it an organized and efficient working space. One very helpful strategy is to

> ### Planning and arranging resources
>
> - Collect all existing resources together.
> - Throw out all those which are incomplete and/or inappropriate.
> - Gather together new/necessary resources.
> - Sort into categories which fit the arrangement of the room.
> - Label by object, catalogue picture, word (possibly label resource *and* location).
> - Locate resources on accessible, open shelving.
> - Train children to locate and return all resources themselves.

give children a 'five-minute warning'. If children are told that they have five minutes before they are asked to stop what they are doing, then it not only gives them the opportunity to start clearing away, but it also gives them time to finish off or to stop an activity at a point which is more appropriate to *them,* rather than instantly because the teacher has found 'we're already late for assembly'.

The outdoor area

The outdoor area is a critical part of the learning environment for children. If we return to the suggestion that the school environment should mirror the successful learning environment of the pre-school child's experiences, then discovering and exploring out of doors clearly offers children new and exciting experiences to stimulate their interest and arouse their curiosity. All too often in school settings, the outdoor learning environment has been reduced to a playground, and what this actually means in practice is that children are sent out of doors simply to let off steam. Even designated outdoor learning areas are sometimes seen this way, and not viewed 'as a combined learning environment worthy of as much thought, effort and capital as the indoor learning environment' (Bilton 1994: 35).

A good early years curriculum acknowledges the value of a learning environment both indoors and outdoors, and should provide for the flow of learning between the two environments. The highly informative ILEA (1990: 6) document, *A Curriculum for Young Children: Outdoor Play*, identifies three different ways of linking the indoor and outdoor environments:

1 the inside can be *transferred* outside – that is elements from the inside are physically moved outside – like rebuilding the home corner outdoors;

2 the provision is *linked* or *paralleled* – for instance, inside water play using tubes and bottles to move water can be paralleled outside using guttering, drainpipes and buckets;

3 an outside activity can be *contrasted* with an activity indoors – small scale painting inside can be contrasted with the use of large sheets of paper and decorating brushes outside.

Designing an outdoor area

Clearly, the design of an outdoor learning environment will be dependent on whether or not there is direct access to the outdoors from the classroom and what opportunities exist outside. Having said that, most classrooms could make better use of the available space, such as it is, than they currently do. It is important to explore the possibilities and to take on board whatever is feasible while lobbying for greater provision.

An outdoor learning environment should have:

A landscape with

- grassed areas and hard surface areas
- tracks using different surfaces, e.g. bricks, cobble stones
- shaded areas and sunlit areas
- places to run and places to sit
- areas to cultivate and areas which encourage natural habitats
- trees, shrubs, bushes, flowers and vegetables
- animals and birds to care for.

Areas to encourage the development of gross motor skills

- swings and ropes
- slides
- climbing frames
- mats to jump on or over
- structures for balancing and jumping between (all sited on appropriate safe surfaces)
- bicycles and tricycles
- wagons and wheelbarrows to push and pull
- scooters
- bouncing and rocking equipment (and pathways to travel on without interrupting the activities of other children).

Activities which encourage fine motor development

- balls and beanbags
- hoops

- quoits
- wood area
- creative area
- small sand and water play.

Resources which encourage exploration and discovery

- construction materials
- sand pit/tray(s)
- water tray(s)
- role-play props
- roadways and play mats
- design and creative materials
- unstructured materials
- music and rhythm materials

(some teachers acquire large carpets which can be put on concrete outside the classroom to enable children to sit and work).

Resources which encourage imagination and expression

- drapes for hide-aways
- a garden shed
- boxes and crates
- masks, cloaks, hats and shoes
- puppets
- an old boat
- large wheels and long ropes.

Storage
- equipment and resources need to be stored so that children can be involved in getting things out and putting them away for themselves.

Safety
- the play area must be fenced off and any entrances should be fitted with safety hooks.

The weather!
- not as bad as we sometimes imagine (just think how relatively few play-times are lost to bad weather). The provision of a covered veranda – preferably wide enough to allow the use of wheeled toys – should protect the children from both extremes of temperature.

The role of the adult
- adults should work with children outdoors in just the same ways as they do indoors. They are there to facilitate, question, respond and extend

children's learning. It is not a time merely for the 'supervision' of behaviour.

Eliminating the little things

In the course of a school day, there are many little things about which children interrupt teachers and waste their valuable professional time. It is useful to write down all the things which cause children to interrupt and which can become agitating. Things like 'my pencil's blunt'; 'can I go to the toilet?'; 'we've run out of green paint'; 'I need some more glue'. Having written these down, it is easier to devise ways of eliminating the interruptions and put classroom time aside to address the issues. This can be a fascinating theme for a staff meeting, when solutions can be jointly constructed.

If children learn to manage the little things in the learning environment, then it can save them, and their teachers, very valuable time. The important thing is to identify what these 'little things' are and then to set about systematically teaching the children to address them themselves. Given time and practice, the youngest children are perfectly cabable of mixing paints or sharpening pencils. Creating time for children to learn these skills can require a changed attitude of mind for some teachers. It means providing the resources to enable children to manipulate them easily – appropriately sized and shaped pencil sharpeners for example. It also means allowing children the time and opportunity to find out for themselves that too much water means their pictures look 'wishy-washy'. To become independent, children need to be taught certain skills and then given time to practise them. It is up to the teacher to set time aside in order to show children how to tie each other's aprons, cut paper, find a new book, etc. Showing children once is, of course, never enough. Experiences like these need repetition, building into the day – perhaps at whole-class time or sharing time – so that the children are constantly reminded of the classroom expectations and how to go about looking after themselves. As with many other classroom issues, time invested here will save time later on. In this instance, the time it will save is teacher time, which can then be spent on the valuable business of teaching rather than 'servicing'. Children feel a great sense of pride and personal achievement when they manage themselves and do not feel they have to consult an adult. The important thing is that children are taught the skills and strategies for independence and are then given opportunities to practise and use them. It is important, too, that the children's efforts are seen as valuable parts of the learning process.

But accidents do happen. Should paint splash on the floor or the water tray spill over, then valuable adult time can be wasted if it is the classroom expectation that it is an adult who clears it up. This is also something that, given appropriate training, children are perfectly capable of doing for themselves. The teacher simply needs to ensure that children have the 'wherewithal' to clear up. It is helpful if, close to those areas which are prone to getting messy, there is a range of equipment for clearing up. Near the water tray, for example, there should be a mop and bucket and sponges; near the sand tray, a broom and dustpan and brush; near the painting table, more sponges, clothes and a supply of paper towels! It helps enormously if, where appropriate, these are child-sized. It helps the children to manipulate the equipment so much more easily and it gives a clear message that this is the province of the children and not something which an adult automatically manages on their behalf.

Involving children in making decisions

I suggested earlier that it can be beneficial for children to be involved in decisions about space and resources as much as is possible. We all know that, given a sense of ownership and a feeling of responsibility about something, we are likely to take more interest and effort in maintainting it. But there are other important reasons why involving children can be of value to them and their teachers.

Involving children:
- gives opportunities for real-life problem-solving
- encourages them to maintain something which they have planned
- enables them to have an element of control over their own learning environment
- leads to the development of organization as a life skill
- gives them a sense of responsibility/self-esteem
- encourages cooperation and collaboration between them and adults
- enables the teacher to see things from the children's perspective.

Children can be involved in planning and arranging:
- the use of space
- the naming of work areas
- the selection of resources
- the categorizing of resources
- the sorting of resources
- the labelling of resources
- the location of resources.

Reviewing the use of space and resources

The design and management of a learning environment is an ongoing exercise. It requires both children and adults to review continuously the classroom as a learning environment and to be given opportunities for suggesting ways in which improvements can be made. The following are useful questions which teachers can ask children – and themselves:

Space

- Do children have room to move about the classroom without interfering in other children's activities?
- Is there space for children to engage in active learning?
- Is there space for a child to sit alone or with a friend as well as in a small group or in a large group?
- Is there space for a child to be quiet as well as to be interactive?

Resources

- Can a child access resources without interfering with the activities of the other children?
- Are the resources clearly visible?
- Do the resources get put back in their right place?
- Are there enough resources for everyone's needs?

Management

- How often are adults interrupted with queries which are not to do with teaching and learning?
- What is the nature of those interruptions?
- Do the children know what to do if paint/paper/glue runs out?
- Do the children know how to sharpen pencils?
- Do the children know what to do if they need aprons/shoes tied?
- Do the children know what to do if things are spilt?
- Do the children know what to do with finished work?
- Do the children know what to do when they have finished an activity?

Establishing independence

Encouraging children to be independent can take time, but it is time wisely spent. It is very hard to plan a teaching day where adults can spend quality time with individuals or groups of children if the rest of the class are not able to operate independently. It may well be that, rather than begin teaching the curriculum from day one, that teachers could spend the early days of a term or year teaching independence. Time can be put aside so that children are taught to find and replace resources, to mix paint, to sharpen pencils, to move from one activity to the next without recourse to an adult (see Chapter 9 for further details). The role of the adult during this time is to facilitate and support this growing independence. Teachers need to have the time to show children how to do something or to remind them where to find something. This is best achieved if the teacher has not planned to spend this time teaching the curriculum as any attempt to teach individuals or groups while children do not have independence is likely to lead to frustration. Establishing whole-class independence – and seeing this as valuable teaching and learning in its own right – will be of long-term benefit to subsequent teaching and learning of the curriculum. When children are independent learners, teachers gain quality time for their own planned activities.

Teaching and learning independence is probably best achieved if children are engaged initially in self-chosen activities. This leaves the teacher free to concentrate on supporting independence rather than anything else. Once children are independent, teacher-initiated activities can be gradually introduced, so that the teacher is able to observe if children can sustain their independence while being required to work at certain prescribed tasks in the course of the day. The teacher still needs to leave sufficient breathing space for herself to remind and support the children when they come for help unnecessarily. When independence is established as a part of class-room life, then the full range of teacher-intensive, teacher-initiated and child-initiated activities can be introduced. This does not mean that the children will never again interrupt the teacher, but the number of times this occurs should be dramatically reduced; the children will feel responsible for their own learning and the teacher will be able to get on with the business of teaching.

Conclusion

Independent learners are a necessary part of classroom life. There are too many children in a class for a teacher to be able to teach all of them directly, all of the time, and it is inevitable that the children will spend a large part of their classroom experience working alone. As we shall see in the next chapter, this is not only necessary but also desirable. Children working together, without adult supervision, is an important part of the curriculum, for when children work alongside their peers they develop many different skills and understandings. Learning to collaborate and cooperate is a life-long process and it is crucial that children have the opportunity to rehearse these skills when they are young. Chapter 6 is concerned with the importance of children working and learning with others; it examines the place of talk in the early years curriculum and challenges some established notions about group work.

6

COLLABORATION AND COOPERATION

The importance of talking and working with others

Introduction

One of the most important elements of an environment appropriate for young learners is the provision of opportunities for children to talk together, and with adults, as they work. There is now a powerful consensus about the centrality of talk to learning, a consensus brought about by the powerful findings of studies of language in the home and at school, including the Bristol Study 'Language at home and at school' directed by Gordon Wells (1981, 1986), the research studies of Barbara Tizard and Martin Hughes (1984) and the work of the National Oracy Project. Studies such as these confirm that talking things through is an essential method by which we all make sense of our experience. Vygotsky (1962) noted how young children solve practical tasks with the help of their speech as well as their eyes and hands and use language as a way of sorting out their thoughts. At first, language and action are fused together in this way, and that is why young children are often heard talking to themselves when they are engaged in an activity. Eventually, language and action become separated and the activity can be represented in the medium of words (Bruner 1985).

The realization of the impact of language on thought and learning has had two significant influences on classroom practice. The first concerns talk between the child and the teacher:

to be most helpful, the child's experience of conversation should be in a one-to-one situation in which the adult is talking about matters that are of interest and concern to the child ... or about activities in which the child and adult engage together.

(Wells 1985: 44)

The second influence concerns children and their peers and a response to the assertion that:

collaborative talk not only facilitates the task, it also empowers the learner. Indeed ... it has the potential for promoting learning that exceeds that of almost any other type of talk.

(Chang and Wells 1988: 97)

Communication with adults

In the preschool years, talking and learning go hand in hand. Children communicate with adults and their siblings and peers about things that are of interest and concern to them. The strategies which children have developed for actively making sense of their experiences have, as we have seen, been highly effective. Yet once children go to school, this model of active learning through talk is not always emulated. Instead, children very often meet the vestiges of the learning-by-listening model of teaching, with few opportunities to engage in the kinds of dynamic interaction which might bring about the quality of learning described above. Tizard and Hughes (1984) point out that comparisons between conversations at home and in the nursery reveal how differently children can behave in two settings, and that in some cases 'it is hard to believe it is the same child who is talking'. Teachers talk to children in two different contexts: first, as individuals or as members of a small group and, second, as members of the whole class.

Talking to individuals

Conversations with individual children are a critical part of the teacher's repertoire of teaching strategies. It is important that these conversations are not one-sided – that is, on the teacher's side. If teachers do most of the talking or ask most of the questions, then they leave children few opportunities to express their own ideas or raise their own questions. The studies of conversations in the home environment, cited above, reveal that what is characteristic about these conversations is that they are spontaneous and arise from activities in which one or both of the participants are engaged. The conversations are, therefore, given meaning by the context in which they occur.

It may seem to teachers that such learning is not possible in a context where one child shares the attention of their teacher with some thirty or so other children. It is, of course, difficult to be spontaneous when there is a planned curriculum to follow. However, because time is precious, it is vital that teachers examine the interactions they do have with individual children to assess which characteristics of successful interactions in the home are mirrored in the classroom. Wells (1985: 68) believes that it is neither desirable nor necessary that the style of learning between home and school should change significantly:

> The strategies that children have developed for actively making sense of their experiences have served them well up to this point; they should now be extended and developed, not suppressed by the imposition of routine learning tasks for which they can see neither a purpose nor a connection with what they already know and can do.

Talking to individual children gives the teacher the opportunity to:

- build a relationship;
- know what they understand and think about an activity or experience;
- know what they understand or can do in a certain situation;
- answer questions;
- extend their knowledge and understanding through information, suggestion and questioning.

It is this depth of knowledge about a child that enables a teacher to move them through Vygotsky's 'zone of proximal development' (see Chapter 1). Unless teachers know each child's present levels of understanding, then they cannot know what their potential might be.

Traditionally, teachers have used questioning as a strategy to discover whether children have either listened to or learnt the information which the teacher has imparted. Many studies of primary classes (e.g. Galton *et al.* 1980; Stodolsky *et al.* 1981; French and Maclure 1983) have revealed that during interactions with their teachers, children are required to recall a tremendous number of 'facts'. The teacher asks a question to which she knows the answer and to which she wants children to given a confirmatory response. Questions are not used to enquire into the wide range of understandings which children might hold, but to elicit the one particular fact which the teacher wants to confirm. In classrooms, the questions raised by teachers overwhelm – and in some cases completely obliterate – the number raised by children. By and large, this is because the teacher initiates the topic of conversation and is, therefore, in control of the ensuing debate. The conversation follows the agenda of the teacher, it is instigated for the purposes of the teacher and the children learn to adopt the passive role of responder rather than sustain their active role of enquirer (Rowland 1984).

When teachers talk to individual children, it is important to adopt a style of questioning which extends their understanding and leads them to new ways of thinking for themselves. Questioning which is closed and which requires children to give a correct answer can inhibit the teacher–pupil relationship, because the children sense that, in a way, the teacher is trying to catch them out. Do they know this, or not? Were they listening, or not? Does this need repeating, or not? Questions which prescribe answers are just as limiting as checklists which prescribe actions. In both cases, teachers will only learn what their chosen strategy allows children to reveal. Conversations in which the teacher knows the answer and the child does not establish a power base for the teacher which inhibits the kind of collaborative construction of meaning which is mutually relevant. It is this willingness on the part of the teacher to negotiate, says Wells, that gives them the confidence to explore their own understandings. Knowledge has to be 'constructed afresh by each individual knower' and teachers cannot rely on the transmission of their own knowledge as a strategy for successful learning by the child.

Dillon (1981) claims that excessive questioning makes pupils dependent and passive. In order to make effective use of what is at its best a very valuable teaching strategy, it is as well for teachers to be aware of practices which reduce the effectiveness of questioning as a tool in the repertoire of the effective teacher. In their book *Questioning*, Brown and Wragg (1993: 18) suggest that the following are common errors in questioning, and their list is useful in raising teacher awareness of their own questioning strategies:

- asking too many questions at once
- asking a question and answering it yourself
- asking questions only of the brightest or most likeable
- asking a difficult question too early
- asking irrelevant questions
- always asking the same type of questions
- not indicating a change in the type of question
- not using probing questions
- not correcting wrong answers
- ignoring answers
- failing to see the implications of answers
- failing to build on answers.

Talking to individual children is a skilled activity and one which, if the chosen strategies are appropriate, is vital for the teacher's knowledge and understanding of the child and the child's knowledge and understanding of a whole world of things.

Talking to the whole class

Early years teachers almost always spend some time in the school day talking to the whole class. These whole-class times, or 'carpet' times as they are often called, may be at the start of the day, at lunch time, at the end of the afternoon or before the start of a session. Very often this carpet time will include a 'discussion' about work that has been completed or is about to be undertaken. Discussions such as these are often characterized by teachers illiciting information from children about what they know about or have learnt about a given subject. Research into this kind of dialogue frequently reveals less of a discussion and more of a diatribe. Barnes and his colleagues (1969) noted that teachers usually retain the initiative throughout, by a strategy of asking questions and monopolizing the commentary on the answers that are given. My own classroom research with my colleague Carol Boulter confirms these findings. The infant teachers we observed undertaking different whole-class sessions showed them to be concerned with getting the 'right' answer, given by the 'right' child, in the 'right' way.

The 'right' answer
Our video transcripts revealed that 'discussions' were dominated by the teachers' agenda. There was no evidence that they were trying to find out what the children understood as a starting point for the discussions or for planning the future curriculum. They told us they were concerned with finding out what the children had learned from the activities they had set up, rather than finding out what they already knew about and would bring to the experience. They used the technique of questioning to elicit the 'right' answer – that is, the answers that were in their own heads. They did this by rejecting answers which were deemed to be 'correct'. In doing this, they sometimes created conceptual confusion in the children, in that they frequently offered no explanation as to why an answer was accepted or rejected. Therefore, children who had been 'guessing the answer in the teacher's head' had no idea why they were either wrong *or* right.

The 'right' child
The teachers further controlled the 'discussions' by insisting that children put their hands up to answer questions. This is common practice of course, but it does give the teacher a controlling mechanism.

As classroom gender studies show, teachers use questioning as a way of including and involving miscreant boys – usually sitting at the back of the class – in an attempt to pre-empt antisocial behaviour (see, for example, Stanworth 1981; Spender 1982; Clarricoates 1983). The 'right' child was, therefore, the one named by the teachers, and the naming of the child seemed fairly dependent on one of two factors. Either they were children who were not attending – and, indeed, in every case but one they were boys. Or they were children to whom the teachers turned in exasperation or expectation to give them the 'right' answer – and in *every* case this was a girl.

The 'right' way

In their drive towards the right answer, the teachers were not prepared to be diverted. Consequently, if children asked questions or made comments which seemed likely to lead them 'off course', they were ignored or rejected. There are also examples, particularly in our transcripts of science lessons, of missed opportunities to start from the children's concerns or interests. The 'right' way meant keeping to the teacher's agenda and meeting their intended objectives to cover a certain aspect of the planned curriculum. Such whole-class sessions became the expression and exploration not of the children's ideas but of the teacher's. They were in marked contrast to the claims for cognitive development, made by Alexander *et al.* (1992: para. 90), that 'Whole class teaching is associated with higher order questioning, explanations and statements, and these in turn correlate with higher levels of pupil performance'.

Perhaps at this point it is necessary to remind ourselves that the discussion paper *Curriculum Organisation and Classroom Practice in Primary Schools* (Alexander *et al.* 1992) was written primarily about children and their experiences at Key Stage 2. A booklet written in response to this by Tricia David, Audrey Curtis and Iram Siraj-Blatchford (1992) – and dubbed the report of the 'Three Wise Women' – comprehensively dismissed the use of this strategy with nursery and infant children, stating that there was inconclusive evidence of its effectiveness and, indeed, there was evidence of the *ineffectiveness* of such whole-class strategies for the early years (Willes 1983; Stevenson 1987).

In her doctoral thesis, Carol Boulter (1992) challenges the pattern of discourse adopted by teachers who attempt to provide for individuals through focused questions to each child while the rest of the class listen. Her study of classroom practice in which the teacher was committed to allowing children's ideas to be heard, and where the class jointly collaborated to investigate questions, demonstrates that it is possible to break with the default way of controlling classroom talk and to mediate the child's voice, thus avoiding the syndrome of the right answer, right child, right way. The teacher in this study gave whole class discussion an explicit framework and saw her role as one of guiding the discussion and summarizing it at key moments. The teacher's questions were almost always to do with helping the discussion along, or clarifying something said by a child, rather than seeking to illicit the right answer. In this way, the children's own conceptual ideas were deliberated and both they and their teacher became clearer about individual understandings and thought processes.

According to Tizard and Hughes (1984: 14), school conversations show 'how full of traps the deliberate process of aiding intellectual growth can actually be, and how this process can indeed be counterproductive'. Clearly, if talk between teachers and children is such a critical part of the education process, then teachers must ensure that the strategies they use extend rather than inhibit children's learning.

Communicating with other children

Children talking with each other to learn is, as we have seen, a relatively new phenomenon in schools. The term 'oracy' was coined in the mid-1960s by Andrew Wilkinson to stress the importance of the language skills of listening and talking. These separate functions are now enshrined in the jargon of the National Curriculum as 'speaking and listening'. Whichever nomenclature is used, oracy now has a distinctive place in the curriculum, not only as a medium of learning in all subjects, but as a subject in its own right – as an aspect of language competence which is taught alongside the traditionally recognized skills of reading and writing.

If children are to have meaningful conversations with each other, then they need to be placed in learning situations which facilitate this. Since the early 1970s, primary school classrooms have generally been organized with children sitting around tables in groups of four to seven (Bealing 1972). The Plowden Report (CACE 1967) is usually seen as having legitimized the move towards a more relaxed classroom atmosphere where children no longer sat in rows waiting passively for the teacher to instruct them. The work of Galton and Williamson (1992) shows that the reasons for the change may have been more complex and varied than simply the desire to promote group teaching and collaborative work. But it is the fostering of collaboration between children which teachers usually give as the prime justification for group seating arrangements.

Example 5: Planning for talk

A teacher had identified the following learning outcomes for a lesson:

(a) the children will make predictions and justify them.
(b) the children will use appropriate scientific and mathematical vocabulary.

The activity entailed guessing the contents of several birthday presents which had been wrapped in various colourful pieces of birthday wrapping paper. The five 4-year-old children were sitting on the carpet with the presents in a pile in front of them. The activity had tremendous potential. The children were eager to pick up, feel and shake the presents and a lot of valuable language was already being used as the teacher settled down to the activity. Instead of this language being harnessed and extended, the children were told to stop talking. They were then told that they could look but not touch, and the teacher proceeded to lift each present in turn and ask for the children's predictions about its contents, which the teacher recorded. The children were not asked to justify their responses. Indeed any justification – 'Perhaps you think that because it's hard ... square ... noisy ... ' – was given by the teacher. By the end of the activity (there were seven presents), the children had made their predictions but had not had the opportunity to justify them, even when they had changed their minds following peer pressure. The teacher had used a great deal of mathematical and scientific language, but the children had used virtually none. The worst aspect for the children was that they were told that they would not find out if they were 'right' until the next day ... when all the other children had done the 'guessing' part of the tasks. This session was an example of the rich potential for language being squandered. The possibilities for use of language were excellent, the children were motivated and the task was highly appropriate. However, the teaching strategies used rendered all that potential null and void.

A number of major studies, however, have highlighted inconsistencies between the way in which children are seated and the tasks in which they are engaged. The ORACLE Project (Galton *et al.* 1980), the Junior School Project (Mortimore *et al.* 1986), Tizard and co-workers' (1988) research in infant schools, PRISMS (Curriculum Provision in Small Primary Schools) (Galton and Patrick 1990) and the Primary Education in Leeds Project (Alexander 1992) all reveal similar findings – that children may sit in groups around tables, but they usually work on tasks as individuals.

Grouping children

Grouping as an organizational strategy

Managing large classes calls for creative thinking on the part of the teacher. Even at the level of moving children around the classroom and the school, it can be helpful to have children organized in small units. If children are in groups with a collective label such as 'red' group, 'scarf' group or 'leek' group (or any one of the 1001 names that groups are given!), some potentially chaotic times such as lining up, getting to assembly and moving round the apparatus can be managed in a more calm and orderly way.

Grouping as an educational strategy

Many teachers feel that children benefit from the sense of belonging to a group, that it gives children security and offers them opportunities to respond collectively and cooperatively. This rationale is essentially social and emotional and does not necessarily fulfil the wider learning needs that the group may have. There is an important difference between children sitting together *in* groups and working together *as* a group. Because research shows that many children sit in groups but work as individuals, it suggests that some teachers may group children for the purposes of their own planning rather than the purposes of children's learning. Rather than plan for the individual needs of a class of thirty children or more, the teacher plans work for each of, say, four groups and the children are given tasks which are planned for the whole group to do, but which basically require each child to work as an individual. Some typical examples of such tasks would be completing individual maths work books, filling in a worksheet or preparing a design for a model.

To maximize the potential of children being grouped together, tasks should require children to collaborate and cooperate. Children who sit together but do not share a common purpose for communication are likely to be distracted by sitting close together (Hastings and Schweiso 1995). This is when talk veers on to topics such as television and pet rabbits. Tasks need to be planned so that children share, discuss, argue, rationalize, find solutions and come to decisions together. If children benefit from speaking when formulating concepts, then it is also vital that they talk with peers who will listen and deliberate their ideas. Thus, if children are to benefit from social interaction, the skills of listening need to be taught alongside the skills of talking. Only if both speaking and listening are a planned part of the curriculum will the social, linguistic and cognitive benefits of group work give an educational rationale for children sitting and working in this context.

A rationale for grouping children

Practical (for the teacher)

- time management
- ease of planning
- use of scarce resources.

Developmental (for the child)

Social

- recognizing strengths and weaknesses in self and others
- learning to give and take
- respecting the opinions of others
- handling conflict
- developing management/leadership skills.

Linguistic

- communicating for a purpose
- articulating thoughts, ideas and opinions
- using different kinds of talk for a purpose.

Cognitive

- the development of critical attitudes (to evidence, opinion, etc.)
- increase in powers of reasoning
- opportunities to hypothesize, question and develop ideas collaboratively
- maximizing thinking power (two heads are better than one)
- the opportunity to go beyond the information given and generate new questions.

The appropriateness of grouping young children

Putting children in groups so that they collaborate is not necessarily appropriate across the full early years age range. Younger children will not cooperate simply because it is in the teacher's plans. Yet young children will cooperate and collaborate with commitment when they see the need to do so. Observations of young children working on construction or in the home corner reveal just how collaborative they can be. It is important that teachers of our youngest children question the reasoning behind any grouping which is teacher-directed. Do young children need to be in groups in order that there is a system for effective classroom management? The answer may well be 'yes'. Do these 4- and 5-year-olds need to be in groups for educational reasons? The answer is almost certainly 'no'. I must stress here the difference between being 'put in a group' and working alongside other children. We have already seen how crucial it is for children to work alongside and learn from other children. I am challenging the need for young children to be *put* in a group of children *in order to* work collaboratively. To encourage cooperation between young children, teachers should plan activities and work areas which encourage spontaneous interactive learning opportunities and in which children see a purpose in talking together and working together.

Planned grouping

In order to maximize the learning potential of a collaborative activity, the criteria for grouping older children need to reflect the purpose of the task in which the group are to engage. There are times when it is beneficial for children with similar interests to work together to inspire and motivate each other. There are times when children of similar ability will benefit from the collaborative exploration of a shared challenge. If the choice of group is to reflect the nature and purpose of the task, then the implication of this is that groupings will *change* in order for that match to be achieved.

Fixed grouping

Because children have different needs at different times, the teacher has to plan for those needs to be met, not only through the selection of a task, but through the social context in which the task takes place. Grouping which remains fixed and inflexible does not acknowledge the needs of the developing child. Children develop in highly individualistic ways and although patterns of development can be similar, children make spurts and reach plateaux in ways which are highly idiosyncratic. Their development cannot be catered for by decisions about their ability which remain the same for any period of time, particularly if that decision is held as constant across all subject areas or areas of learning. The needs of any small group of children, however similar their ability at any given time, will not be constant from day to day. Because four children are ready to learn about the concept of 'more than' at the same time, it does not necessarily follow that they will come to understand 'the difference between' at the same time. If different rates of learning mean that children have different learning needs *within* one subject, how much more will those needs vary *across* subjects.

Yet sometimes children are grouped with the same children for *all* subjects. Their needs may originally have been assessed in one subject, and then presumed to be similar in everything else. How rarely this is the case. Children have such a range of skills, talents and understandings, that to suppose that one child can be 'above average' in all curriculum areas while another is consistently 'below average' is to make inaccurate not to mention improbable assessments of children's abilities. Children usually perform according to the expectations of those who influence them. Tell them they're a 'leek' (one of my bright ones) and they'll perform like a leek. Tell them they're a 'cabbage' (my slow learners) and they'll perform like a cabbage, even though some children know that given half a chance they could perform like a leek in PE or technology or scientific investigation.

Labelling children in fixed ability groups can inhibit all manner of opportunities for development. It can restrict the opportunity to shine, gain confidence from and develop in those areas in which the child has strengths. It can also restrict the opportunity to work with a range of peers from whom the child can learn and to whom the child can teach a variety of things. Bringing together children who have the same learning needs at a given time is a constructive use of time. Constraining children to work with the same group of children consistently might, at best, inhibit development and, at worst, destroy a child's belief in their ability to do anything.

Flexible grouping

Effective grouping recognizes the ever-changing needs of children and the necessity to be flexible in planning the curriculum and the context in which that curriculum takes place. It means that children are brought together because they have similar needs at that moment in time. Knowledge of those needs comes from observations and conversations which identify every child's stage of development and provide clear evidence on which to base diagnostic assessments and future plans. Teachers need to be flexible in their short-term planning so that whatever they discover about children and their development can be incorporated into weekly and daily reviews of every child's needs.

This may sound a tall order, but it is less complex when seen in the light of the fact that, for educational purposes, children do not need to do group work all of the time. If children sit in groups but work as individuals, then it is irrelevant whether or not they sit at a table with children of the same ability. This kind of grouping is an organizational arrangement and the group may be selected for any number of reasons that may have little to do with the curriculum. There are times when children *need* to work alone. If, however, the purpose of an activity is that the children will learn with and from each other, then it is necessary for the teacher to make decisions about which children should work together to make this an effective learning experience. Children may be set a task to work at as a group, independent of the teacher, or they may work with the teacher or another adult, addressing a specific learning need. The important point is that the activity is relevant at that time to those children who have been grouped together.

The variabilities of grouping

The groups for which teachers plan can vary in size, composition and permanency. The following is a summary of the key issues about the variabilities of grouping.

The variabilities of grouping

Size

Those who have researched small group work (e.g. Kagan 1988; Fisher 1990) conclude that FOUR is the optimum for effective interaction.

Composition

By age
- often used in vertically grouped classes
- implicit assumption that children of the same age are similar in ability.

By ability
- children often selected on ability in language or maths
- implicit assumption that a child is of the same ability across the curriculum
- implications for teacher expectation and pupil motivation/performance.

By learning needs
- children brought together with those at similar stage of development in a given area because at that time (for maybe one activity) they have similar learning needs.

By mixed ability
- less able children given ideas and explanations by more able peers

- more able children given genuine reasons for demonstrating skills and explaining concepts
- opportunities for children to work with a wide variety of peers.

By friendship
- children motivated by working with those with whom they are happy and confident
- collaboration most likely to be achieved at first by children working with friends.

The range of learning contexts

Group work is clearly only one context for classroom learning. The teacher has a range of options on which to draw:

- whole class
- small group plus teacher
- small group plus another teacher
- small group minus adult
- pair with teacher (adult)
- pair without adult
- individual with adult
- individual alone.

Given the variety of learning situations in any one class and the variety of needs of children as learners, how does the teacher make decisions about which context is most appropriate? Alexander *et al.* (1992) state that the criterion should be 'fitness for purpose' and this is a helpful starting point. It seems logical that any decision made in a classroom should serve the purpose of the activity for which it is chosen. However, it begs the question, whose purpose? The choice of social context in a classroom situation may be the child's, but may be – and I suggest more often is – the teacher's. The following offers a rationale for choosing different social contexts for learning. The suggestions came from a series of inservice sessions with early years teachers.

The child's choice of grouping

What social contexts would the child choose? Unaware of the myriad of learning opportunities presented by their friends, children work alongside other children for different reasons. Young children learn

Purposes of different learning contexts

Whole class

- telling
- imparting knowledge
- enthusing (beginnings)
- sharing (endings).

Small group plus teacher

- differentiation between groups
- time management (class sizes)
- keeping children on task
- individualized questioning
- more opportunities to *listen* to individuals
- opportunities to observe practical work and social interaction
- extending knowledge and understanding
- sharing resources
- safety.

Small group minus teacher

- revision/rehearsal of the familiar
- independent discussion
- collaboration/cooperation (joint outcome).

Pair

- mutual support (response partner)
- shared interest
- motivation (friendships)
- age – older/younger children supporting.

Individual

- child's need for privacy
- individual progress
- pride in ownership
- maximization of concentration.

best in contexts in which they feel secure. Security comes from being familiar with and trusting those who share the learning space. When given the opportunity to work alongside whoever they choose, children do not always work with a special friend. Often their own interest in an activity will determine where they choose to work. But young children do tend to gravitate towards those with whom they are comfortable and confident. Being secure enables children to relax, to experiment, to take risks and to stimulate their own learning. Alongside other children they may ask questions or sound out ideas which, in the company of an adult – however supportive – they may feel inhibited to do. Much research on small group work (Barnes and Todd 1977; Jones 1988; Phillips 1988; Reid *et al.*1989) has shown that children are more likely to generate exploratory questions, hypotheses and explanations on their own than when a teacher is present. Working alongside someone with whom you feel secure is a powerful motivating factor. Just think how many adults do not go along to evening classes or join a sports club unless they go with a friend for moral support. Being with someone we like and trust adds to our feelings of enjoyment and security and this affects our application to the task in hand.

There are times when teachers want or need children to work with specified others and these pairings or groups may cut across friendships or those with whom the the child might instinctively choose to work. Such groupings are valid and valuable. Teachers need children to work together because they are the same or different in their confidence, dominance, gender, age, ethnicity, language competence or ability. But on those occasions when it is possible to enable children to choose their own workmate, this enhances children's learning experiences and increases the possibility of sustained interest and involvement in what they are doing.

Grouping children is a complex business. It is an important part of the decision-making processes of the teacher and is concerned with the differentiation of activities. Given the learning needs of the child, with whom should he or she work and for what purpose? Will the task be best achieved through collaboration? Does the child need the support of an adult? The critical issue is whether the grouping in a classroom is for organizational or educational reasons. It is important that teachers are clear about the two functions of grouping in order that they do not confuse their usage.

Conclusion

Children talk to learn and need to be given many opportunities to talk purposefully to their peers and to adults. Teachers need to ensure that classroom conversations are not one-sided and that children have genuine opportunities to say what they know and what they feel.

When teachers group children for educational reasons, these groupings should be flexible and responsive to the changing needs of children. Young children naturally collaborate and cooperate when they see the need to do so, and they do so particularly when they are engaged in self-initiated activities. The following chapter is concerned with child-initiated learning. It explores the place of play in the early years classroom and asks why teachers can find it hard to justify time for play alongside the rest of the curriculum.

7

THE PLACE OF PLAY

The status of child-initiated experiences

Introduction

No book about early childhood education would be complete without a discussion of the place of play. Any teacher who has been through a training course explicitly designed for the early years will be in no doubt about the place of play in the development of young children's learning. High-quality nursery provision has a range of exciting and innovative play opportunities for children as the bedrock of their planned curriculum. Yet this is not usually the case once children enter the world of statutory schooling. Research shows that there is an immense gap between the rhetoric and the reality of play being at the heart of the early years curriculum. While infant teachers quite commonly talk about the value of play, they frequently do not find a place for it in their classroom practice (Pascal 1990; Ofsted 1993b). As this book is primarily concerned with the implementation of an appropriate early years curriculum within the constraints of the National Curriculum, this chapter will focus on the place of play in the early years classroom, alongside the National Curriculum, and its subjects.

A definition of play

Part of the dilemma is that not everyone considers 'play' to mean the same thing. There is no single definition of play and, therefore, playful activities in one form or another have been open to interpretation in different ways. There is, however, no shortage of definitions and no shortage of writers and practitioners who have put forward a theory of what elements constitute 'play'. For a detailed synopsis of the main theories, I refer the reader to Tina Bruce's (1991) book, *Time to Play in Early Childhood Education*; this book forms the basis of much of the writing in this chapter. Bruce offers a range of examples.

1 *Recreation theory* proposes that play somehow redresses the balance of time spent on work; that play is acknowledged as an appropriate activity for young children but not the same as, and certainly not as important as, work. In this way, play is sometimes used as a reward, as a 'carrot' at the end of a period of work when the child has the opportunity to engage in something of their own choosing once the work for the teacher is finished.

2 *Excess energy theory* sees play as an acceptable way for children to let off steam and this separates 'worktime' from 'playtime'. This theory has given a framework to the infant school day – and, indeed, to junior and secondary education too – which has changed little over the years. 'Playtime' is given value in that it releases pent-up energies and prepares children to knuckle down to the more static learning experiences to which they will return.

3 *Recapitulation theory* suggests that play reflects the cultural environment in which the child grows up. Play is seen as being deeply embedded in children's personal experiences and a reflection of the influences of children's environments and the significant people within them.

4 *Practice or preparation theory* suggests that play helps children to prepare for adult life, by letting them practise and explore what they need to be able to do as adults. Young children engage in role play which mimics, often with devastating accuracy, the behaviours of adults who are significant in their lives.

5 *Play as pleasure theory* sees play as 'a source of pleasure, and is in no way dependent upon the anticipated results of this activity'(Buhler 1937, in Bruce 1991: 31). This theory emphasizes the importance of play as process, a view strongly held by Bruner (1977: v), who, while not subscribing to the play as pleasure theory, nonetheless asserts that 'Play is an approach to action, not a form of activity'.

6 *Affective theories of play* are child-centred theories of play where children are seen as having control over their actions and their lives. There is an important role for others, both adults and children, in acting as catalysts to the play. In these theories, play is seen as continuing into adult life and leading to a range of cultural and creative activity.

7 *Cognitive development theories* are also child-centred theories but do not stress the importance of play in adult life.

Piaget saw play as the means by which the child unifies experience, knowledge and understanding and comes to control them. Piaget saw young children's free play as developing in a linear way into games with rules rather than into more creative aspects of human experience.

Although Bruner's work emphasizes the value of play as process, he gives structure to what he constitutes as play, which takes it out of the realms of being a 'free' activity. He sees play as games from the start – games such as 'Peek a boo' – and sees activities such as sand, clay, water and dough as being without purpose and lacking intellectual challenge (Bruner 1980). Bruner sees the purpose of play as being preparation for adult life, when children take their place in society.

Vygotsky (1966: 6) sees play as both cognitive and affective, referring to it as 'the leading source of development in preschool years'. Like Piaget, he sees play as having rules, not ones that are formulated in advance, but ones stemming from the situation itself. Because of this, Vygotsky discounts the notion of play as pleasure, citing the playing of sporting games which are 'very often accompanied by a keen sense of displeasure'.

8 *An integrating mechanism.* Tina Bruce has championed a more precise definition of play. Building on the work of Froebel, McMillan and Isaacs, she develops the notion of 'free-flow' play. This process is 'concerned with the way children integrate, use and apply their knowledge'. In *Time to Play*, Bruce (1991) outlines twelve features of free-flow play which help to clarify its definition and help to tease out 'how free-flow play differs from struggle, exploration and practice, or from representation, games and humour' (p. 57):

1 It is an active process without a product.
2 It is intrinsically motivated.
3 It exerts no external pressure to conform to rules, pressures, goals, tasks or definite direction.
4 It is about possible, alternative worlds, which involve 'supposing', and 'as if', which lift players to their highest levels of functioning. This involves being imaginative, creative, original and innovative.
5 It is about participants wallowing in ideas, feelings and relationships. It involves reflecting on and becoming aware of what we know, or 'metacognition'.
6 It actively uses previous firsthand experiences, including struggle, manipulation, exploration, discovery and practice.
7 It is sustained, and when in full flow, helps us to function in advance of what we can actually do in our real lives.
8 During free-flow play, we use the technical prowess, mastery and competence we have previously developed, and so can be in control.

9 It can be initiated by a child or an adult, but if by an adult he/she must pay particular attention to points 3, 5 and 11.
10 It can be solitary.
11 It can be in partnerships, or groups of adults and/or children who will be sensitive to each other.
12 It is an integrating mechanism, which brings together everything we learn, know, feel and understand.

(Bruce 1991: 59–60)

The importance of play

I have noted just a few of the many claims made for the importance of play, yet play still has to fight to maintain its place in the infant classroom. One reason for this may be the undermining of confidence caused by claims that much of the theorizing about the importance of play has been carried out in the absence of any real evidence that play does or does not have the effect and benefits postulated (Smith and Cowie 1991). Bruner (1966), despite his own stance on play as 'practice in mastery' and his belief that being playful is a time when children learn to take important risks and find boundaries as well as freedoms, still wrote of the 'extraordinary dogmatism' that play is beneficial to young children, a view that Sutton-Smith and Kelly-Byrne (1984) have called the 'idealization' of play. Much of the work of the 'early pioneers' of early childhood education (as Bruce refers to them), such as Froebel (1782–1852), McMillan (1860–1931) and Isaacs (1885–1948), can be seen influencing practice in play environments in nurseries and schools in Britain today (see Moyles 1989; Bruce 1991; Smith and Cowie 1991), but their work was based largely on first-hand and anecdotal evidence rather than the kind of 'hard' evidence which is required by formal research methodology. Recently, however, this situation has been addressed, most notably by the empirical study of children's play and play behaviours in the Froebel Blockplay Project (see Gura 1992), which analysed the development of children's block play as an integral part of the whole curriculum. The findings do indeed give us fresh perspectives on many aspects of children's play. Those engaged in the project analysed the development of play at the micro-level and examined the use children make of play to represent some ideas more powerfully than through words. It is a study which demonstrates the crucial role of adults in play and the roles which adults can adopt as researchers as well as practitioners.

Perhaps another reason why play does not hold its place in the infant classroom is because teachers do not have or make the time to gather the kind of observations which would give them the evidence they personally need to be convinced of the importance of play. Let us look at this issue in relation to some of the early theories.

Recreation theory

In recreation theory, play has a different status to work. It does not have the status reflected in Vygotsky's (1966: 92) view that 'a child's greatest achievements are possibly in play'. The status it is given places it firmly in second place behind work. Work is more important because it is controlled by the teacher and must usually be completed before – as some kind of reward – children are allowed to play. This time to play is very often referred to as 'choosing' and this term also signifies the status of the play. It says to children that there are only certain, very limited, times when they have control over their learning experiences and can exercise choice and make decisions. The rest of the time children's experiences are in the control of the teacher and are dominated by the teacher's choices and her decisions. The reason why play is relegated to this position is two-fold. First, teachers actually see play as being less important than work; if they did not, then play would have a different status and a different place in the classroom experience. The argument that there is no time for play shows that play is not seen as process, a way of integrating or consolidating skills and understandings, but as a separate activity, another subject to be added on to all the other subjects that have to be covered.

The second reason for play being relegated in the classroom hierarchy is that play motivates, interests and absorbs children and is ideal for using as a 'carrot' in order to encourage children to finish the possibly less inspiring and motivating tasks set by the teacher. It is also valuable in keeping children out of the teacher's hair while she completes her designated teaching tasks. In this way, children get further messages about the place of play. Not only is it something which is less important than work, but it is also something that the teacher is not particularly interested in because she spends her time working alongside children engaged in tasks which she has initiated. Play is consigned to the corners of the classroom, both in terms of time and space. It is not observed by the teacher and she rarely finds time to participate. Resources are limited and space for play is cramped because space for work is given precedence. Time for play is dependent upon the amount of time in any session before play, PE, television or whichever interruption to the day is next on the timetable. No wonder children come to view play as being subsidiary to work.

Indeed, children also seem to learn very quickly once they enter school that if it is play it cannot be work. Fein (1981) found that children between the ages of 5 and 9 years have very clear ideas about work and play, which can only have been formed from their own experiences. Work is compulsory, done for an adult and is very often done alone. It is subject to judgement and evaluation by others, and has performance criteria – usually right or wrong. Play, on the other hand, is voluntary, it is done for its own sake, often in the company of others, and is subject to judgement by the child. Adelman (1992: 139) sees this division between work and play as part of the influence of the Protestant work ethic in schooling where play is seen as 'a temporary and privileged release from the hard grind of real work, study and training'. Whatever its genesis, the ethic is alive and well and living in classrooms!

Excess energy theory

Children are active learners and the most appropriate curriculum for them is one which offers experiences which involve them in investigation, exploration and play. What an indictment for the infant curriculum then that children need to let off steam. It suggests that children have been passively engaged rather than actively involved, required to sit and listen more than move and do. It is interesting to consider that a 4-year-old in a nursery does not need a playtime, but that a 5-year-old in a reception class does. As we saw in Chapter 5, the development of an outdoor area for learning was seen as an antidote to the passive learning environments so indicative of classrooms at the turn of the century. A properly designed outdoor environment offers children the chance to engage in a whole range of active learning situations, including the many opportunities to develop their physical skills through climbing, rolling, throwing, cycling, pushing and so on. This is not 'letting off steam'; it is a crucial part of educating the whole child, an acknowledgement that physical development cannot be separated from the development of the mind and the emotions. When children work in the outdoor area, this is not a time for teachers to sit back and take a supervisory role; it is a time when adults are engaged as much as children, supporting and guiding children's experiences in the same many and varied ways as they do indoors.

The lack of outdoor provision for children in infant classes is well documented. In recent years there has been a substantial increase in the number of 4-year-olds in primary schools, frequently working in classes alongside children of 5, 6 and 7 years of age. Many studies examining the quality of provision for these young children have revealed very low standards (see Sestini 1987; Thomas 1987; Pascal and Ghaye 1988; Bennett and Kell 1989; Brown and Cleave 1990). The most frequent omission in this provision is that of a properly fenced-off, appropriately equipped outside area. It is easy to see why: outdoor equipment, especially large apparatus with proper surfacing, is not

---

Example 6: Improving provision at playtime

One school has been effective in improving the quality of its children's playtime experiences. The headteacher and staff believed that not only did the children need more quality time, but that it would also encourage adults – teachers, classroom assistants and dinner supervisors – to see their role in this context as going beyond a supervisory one. The adults first learnt and then introduced to the children many old rhymes and playground ditties that have gradually disappeared from children's experience. Because of diminished opportunities to play together, most of these childhood rhymes and songs were unknown to many of the children. The school population comprises children from diverse cultural backgrounds and the songs and rhymes from each of these cultures were unfamiliar to the other children, and experiences needed to be shared. Some children did not want to spend playtime rushing around getting hot and said they would prefer to sit and talk, or engage in activities such as reading, mark-making or construction, so these were provided. Other children wanted to be more active but not necessarily play football. The use of footballs was curtailed on a rota basis and a whole variety of small apparatus such as hoops, ropes, quoits and bean-bags were introduced instead. Because of the interaction by the adults, these did not simply disappear – as had apparently happened on previous occasions – but are used constructively and with clear enjoyment and enthusiasm by children of all ages. The behaviour of the children has improved dramatically. Many more children can engage in purposeful activities at playtime and the relationship between the children and lunch-time supervisors has improved. Not only have these improvements altered the quality of playtimes, but teachers report an improvement in behaviour throughout the rest of the day.

---

cheap. But there is so much more that could be done to develop the outdoor learning environment for young children, which would give them opportunities to play outdoors in constructive, developmental ways (see Chapter 3), and not simply in order to release excess energy.

Given the expense of outdoor areas for learning, infant schools can at least address the quality of the play experiences children have at playtimes in order to make them more positive than they currently are. David Brown (1994: 64) examines the playground as a context for children's learning and claims that 'Play areas provide a setting for a cultural forum within which the children can create and recreate meaning from the sum of their experiences'. Brown reminds us that the opportunities children have for playing together in groups with their peers has declined considerably and that the playground has become all the more important as a context for the learning of certain sorts of behaviours.

Recapitulation theory

The quality and nature of children's play is highly culturally specific. The value and status given, or not given, to play in classrooms is often a reflection of the culture of the school community or the teacher's own cultural conditioning, which cannot accept that if an activity is playful it can also be worthwhile. Janet Moyles (1989: 164) explores the different perceptions of parents, teachers and children towards play activities and concludes that, 'Whatever the difficulties faced by all parties, the child needs the kind of concordance and cooperation that real partnership with parents requires, particularly in relation to the value attached to the child's play'.

Audrey Curtis (1994) examines in greater depth the value of play in different cultures. She describes a recent investigation into the use of the microcomputer in the nursery classroom, noting that parents from Asian cultures are particularly enthusiastic about its use, 'as they frequently have difficulties in accepting the traditional nursery-school curriculum with its opportunities for freedom of choice' (p. 33). Few Western parents, she continues, will admit to giving their children specific toys for pure fun, although she quotes a delightful comment made by an African mother to Rabain-Jamin (1989: 298), who claimed that 'We give toys (to children) to play with. You give them toys to teach, for the future. We feel that children learn better when they are older'.

Whatever views parents hold, it is the responsibility of teachers to explain and exemplify the value of play in the classroom. At the same time, teachers will always need to be sensitive to the experiences of children and the culture from which they come. Not only in order to understand the values and expectations which children may hold, but also to resource the play environment with materials and equipment which will be of value and meaning to children in their everyday lives.

Practice or preparation theory

There are many ways in which young children practise 'being an adult'. Part of this is an exploration of the roles of people whom they know and love. Part of it is being intrigued by what it might be like to be a grown up. Part of it is acting out real experiences and assigning themselves roles in order to play out a situation for real. According to Garvey (1977: 88), some of this kind of play represents 'only salient events in a sequence of action ... Most enactments are clearly created from concepts of appropriate behaviour and are most likely not direct imitations of people'.

A home corner which changes to an office, hospital, shop, bank or submarine, or any of the countless innovative ideas which can be seen in classrooms, should be a constant source of opportunity for children to engage in activity which they perceive prepares them for adult life. The joy of this kind of dramatic play is the fusion of fantasy and reality, of being able to deal with issues in a context that enables children to risk the exploration of a whole range of personal and relevant experiences.

Play as pleasure theory

Most definitions of play include some statement about the necessity for the activity to be pleasurable. In a survey of play literature in 1983, Rubin *et al.* distinguished play using six criteria, the first of which is that play is 'intrinsically motivated'. This suggests that children find play pleasurable enough to want to do it. Bruce's (1991: 42) use of the delicious word 'wallow' in her free-flow 'equation' also signals activity that is giving someone a great deal of pleasure. Moyles (1989: 133) claims that 'Play has its own intrinsic rewards, it is done spontaneously and voluntarily and it is thoroughly enjoyable', and even the Department for Education and Science (as it then was) makes the statement that:

> Play that is well planned and pleasurable helps children to think, to increase their understanding and to improve their language competence ... Teachers know that such experience is important in catching and sustaining children's interests and motivating their learning as individuals and in co-operation with others.
>
> (DES 1989: para. 16)

Affective theories of play

It is the control which children have over play activities which makes them pleasurable, particularly in school. So much of a child's day is spent responding to the direction of the teacher that engaging in play allows them to regain the learning initiative. Vicky Hurst (1994) asserts that children's play links with the ways in which all humans – adults as well as children – come to make personal sense of the world. This is a profoundly controlling state in which to be and gives us some sense of why good-quality play experiences have such an impact on the learning and lives of young children.

Affective theories of play emphasize the importance of the role of others – both adults and children – in acting as catalysts to play. The Froebel Blockplay Project recorded a wealth of valuable examples of ways in which children and adults support and extend each other's play ideas. The research proposal (Gura 1992) looked at three roles which might be adopted by adults in their support of play. These were:

- *laissez-faire,* i.e. children are often left to use the blocks without adults;
- *didactic,* i.e. where tasks are frequently set by adults and adults domi- nate play interaction; and
- *interactionist,* i.e. where adults help and encourage play with an emphasis on adult–child play partnering; in order to do this, 'adults need to know as much as possible about the development of young children, and the context of learning' (Gura 1992: 20).

The *laissez-faire* approach, they conclude, 'tends to leave children where they are'. The didactic approach encourages 'dependency, nar- rowness, a desire to please those in authority, conformity and a lack of creativity, imagination or the ability to create and solve problems'. The interactionist approach 'begins where children are, helping them to use what they know, and to move with them into new knowledge and understanding'. One fascinating finding of the project was that chil- dren adopt the adult model of interaction in adult-absent situations with peers. This, they conclude, implies that adults need to *organize* to be absent (as opposed to doing this by default), as well as to be present.

'Structured' play

There is a significant difference between being a catalyst for an activity and dominating it. The time and place for adult intervention is a finely judged thing. Intervention at the wrong moment can be inter- ference, and all practitioners know that terrible feeling when a wrongly timed question or comment can bring some freely flowing play to an abrupt halt. In the need to justify play as a worthwhile school experience, some writers and practitioners have suggested that the involvement of adults gives weight and credence to a pursuit that would otherwise be too frivolous to take up valuable time. In drawing a distinction between play that is child-initiated and play which is initiated by the teacher, Manning and Sharp (1977) used the phrases 'structured' and 'unstructured' play. This is an unfortunate differen- tial in that it suggests that child-initiated play lacks structure. Even more unfortunate is the assumption that unstructured play is somehow the next step to structured play, that children progress from one to the other, that when they are bored with lack of structure the teacher saves the day by injecting some. To begin with the notion of a linear progression in play is inappropriate. Young children need activities which they initiate to take place alongside, betwixt and between activities which are initiated by adults. Adults have a crucial role in supporting and extending play, but there is a fine line between intervention and interference. The minute an adult has a predetermined task or goal in mind, then the activity cannot be play. It becomes, in my own nomenclature, 'a teacher-initiated' activity (see Chapter 4), along with any task for which a teacher has planned predetermined ends. To conclude, we should remember that in the words of Susan Isaacs (1968: 133), 'play has the greatest value for the young child when it is really free and his own'.

The rhetoric and the reality

I wish now to return to the 'often enormous' gap identified by Chris Pascal (1990) in her study of infant classrooms, between the principles about play which teachers espoused and the reality of practice in their classrooms. While 82 per cent of teachers expressed free/imaginative play as their first curriculum priority in providing a curriculum for the 4-year-olds in their class, in practice they employed a greater number of teacher-directed strategies and were 'less comfortable' with child-directed strategies.

This situation is not new. An investigation into the experiences of 4-year-olds in school by Bennett and Kell (1989) found that only 6 per cent of time was spent in play, while Tizard *et al.* (1988) estimated that top infants in the inner-London schools she and her colleagues observed engaged in play for less than 2 per cent of their time. The situation seems to have worsened as the number of 4-year-olds in school has increased. In 1993, the Office for Standards in Education completed a survey of 88 English primary schools to inspect the work of 141 reception classes; Gura (1992) re-enforced many of the points raised by Pascal's study:

- rarely were schools able to make good provision for outdoor play (para. 16);
- lack of space sometimes meant that access was restricted to other valuable learning activities, for example sand and water (para. 16);
- when the lessons were at their best, the adults (demonstrated) ... their ability to sustain and extend talk and play (para. 22);
- The quality of learning through play presented rather a dismal picture. Fewer than half of the teachers fully exploited the

educational potential of play. In more than a third of schools play was only recreational; it lacked an educational purpose and was usually undertaken only after work had been completed. It was largely ignored by adults but sometimes regarded as a useful time filler when pupils were tiring of the main work. In the poorer classes teachers over-directed work and under-directed play. They used play as a reward for finishing work or as an occupational or holding device. By contrast, in the effective classes play was used positively to develop children's abilities across a wide range of activities. For example, the provision of 'home corners', sand and water play activities which are long standing features of the work with young children were planned into the programme with a sound educational purpose rather than as time fillers (para. 25).

I make no apology for including paragraph 25 in its entirety. In the light of all that has been said in this chapter, we must address how teachers in the 'effective' classes were able to 'use play positively to develop children's abilities across a wide range of activities'.

Raising the status of play

In order to raise the status of play in classrooms, teachers need first-hand experience of its value. They need to make a commitment to it

---

A Charter for Play

1 Acknowledge its unique contribution as a process by which young children learn.
2 Plan for it as an integral part of the curriculum and not an 'added extra'.
3 Facilitate it with appropriate and high-quality provision.
4 Act as a catalyst when intervention is appropriate and a scaffolder when expertise is required.
5 Observe it in order to have first-hand evidence of children's learning.
6 Evaluate it in order to better understand the needs of the learner.
7 Value it through comment and commitment in order for its status in the classroom to be appreciated.
8 Fight for it with rigorous, professional argument in order to bring about deeper understanding and acceptance by colleagues, parents, governors and the community at large.

---

as central to the curriculum for young learners. The Charter for Play, p. 106 may support practitioners and their managers in raising the status of play in early years classrooms.

Play and the National Curriculum

There is nothing in the National Curriculum documentation which explicitly negates, undermines or refutes the value of play in early childhood education. There are, in fact, a number of examples within the programmes of study which positively encourage play as a process of learning. The argument from teachers is one of time. *Because* there is so much to 'cover', then there isn't time for play. Now is the time to reiterate what has been said earlier. To suggest that there is insufficient time for play intimates that play is something extra – it is not. Play is a key process whereby children will gain their knowledge and understanding of science, maths, history and any other of the National Curriculum subjects. The quality of the learning experiences if play is of high quality should be all the greater. If time is finite – as we discovered space to be – then once again priorities have to be established and teachers must use their professional judgement to decide which activities will most enhance young children's learning. If we cannot do it all, then what is best for children? There is sufficient evidence to suggest that the learning opportunities offered through play make it a classroom imperative.

Conclusion

Play is the natural way in which children go about the business of learning. It enables them to integrate and consolidate a wealth of experiences which enhance their cognitive, physical, social and emotional development. It naturally encourages cooperation and collaboration, requires the use of fine and gross motor skills and demands cognitive application. It is pleasurable, but also helps children face pain and sorrow. It is consuming, challenging and motivating. The relevance of play to early years education is unquestionable and its status in the classroom should be assured. In Chapter 8, we look at other situations in which children may have power and control in classrooms and see whether they can be motivated by the negotiation of elements of their learning and their learning environment.

8

THE NEGOTIATED CLASSROOM

Issues of power and control

Introduction

The idea of learning being negotiated is a challenge to any curriculum which prescribes the process and content of experiences without taking into account the current needs and interests of children. A developmentally appropriate curriculum, as described in Chapter 3, is built upon what individual children know and need to know next. It is a curriculum which starts from the child rather than expecting the child to start from the curriculum. It presupposes that children are aware of the purpose of the activities in which they are engaged and are able to make judgements about their value. When teachers see the desirability of motivating children in this way, then the learner is placed in a powerful position. Rather than being a passive recipient of someone else's decision-making and control, the learner is an active participant in the formation of their own classroom experiences. When young children exercise control in classroom situations, it determines the relationship between teacher and learner. The relationship becomes a partnership in which children can negotiate input and outcomes in ways which increase their autonomy and sense of purpose. This does not diminish the role of the teacher but alters it. The idea that learning is controlled by the learner

> presupposes that knowledge is not transmitted directly from the teacher to the learner. It demands that both teacher and learner recognise that the subject matter of learning resides outside their 'circle of intimacy', rather than exclusively in the teacher.
>
> (Rowland 1984: 149)

Being a pupil

Within the first few hours of being in school for the first time, or being in a new class, a young child picks up messages about their role in the classroom and what it is like to have collected their first title in life outside the culturally secure daughter, son, granddaughter, or nephew. The title 'pupil' carries with it attitudes and expectations, learnt from those around the child. 'When you're at school you won't be able to do that'; 'at big school they keep you in at dinnertime if you haven't finished your work'; 'now you're at school you'll learn proper things like sums and writing' – a mass of expectations which usually come in the form of well meaning advice, but which can also carry the undertones of threat.

In this way, children arrive at school with a notion, correct to a lesser or greater extent, about what it means to be a pupil. Children believe they are in school to learn and the teacher to teach. The active role is that of the teacher and the appropriate role for a pupil is to be passive and receive the teaching. Children frequently adopt a role which is quite different from the natural role of competent learner which they have played so successfully in the home. This suggests that children often do not make a link between their learning behaviours in the home and their learning behaviours in school. Why should this be? Perhaps it is because they are simply not given opportunities to engage in these activities often enough to see school as an extension of their previous learning environment. Or perhaps the mere fact that they have to come to a different, separate place to 'learn' implicitly suggests that this was not what they were doing before. Acknowledging young children as competent learners means making the transition from home to school as smooth as possible. It also means sending messages to the children that what they are and what they bring with them by way of knowledge and experience is of value and will affect their classroom life. If children are cut off from their previous success and are expected to behave in ways which are alien to them, then this will exacerbate the myth that being a pupil is different from being a child.

Changing a child into a pupil

When children arrive at school there are a battery of experiences that are designed to change them into pupils. The first of these is often the learning of school routines. These are patterns of behaviour which are designed by teachers and learnt by pupils through the imitation of older pupils or through the understanding of teacher cues. The exhortation to 'wait here for the present ' (Lee 1959) is well known and loved. But there are a range of other demands made of children which can leave them equally bemused. One child was told to 'Go and put those on your peg' and turned to his mum and said miserably, 'But I haven't washed them'. Teachers do not intentionally mislead, but children are being required to absorb a new vocabulary and a series of behaviours at a time when many are at their most vulnerable, having left their parent or carer, maybe for a whole day, maybe for the first time.

For many children, this is also their first experience of being one among many, the first time they may have had to share the time and attention of adults, and this can be difficult. Just when you need someone to reassure you about a whole host of things which are new and bewildering, you cannot find anyone who has the time. Then when you want to say something – when there is an adult, a 'teacher', sitting close by within asking distance – you meet the most entrenched routine of all, putting your hand up. Sinclair and Coulthard (1975) call this 'bidding', which is an excellent description. The children bid for the teacher's time by raising their hands in response to the demand to do so. It is a request to hold the floor and have the teacher's attention. Putting up your hand demands an under-standing of two basic rules: one, that in order to speak to the teacher, this is what you need to do; two, that there are times when you can talk to other children and times when you cannot, and this is one when you cannot unless you are told you can, in which case you must but only when you're told!

Because the rules and routines are bewildering, many children resort to imitation. Sometimes that imitation is of other children who have been in the class longer or who have simply 'cottoned on' faster. Children offer responses 'that clearly enough imitate those that have recently been offered and have seemed to please the teacher well enough to get positive feedback' (Willes 1983: 186). Sometimes the imitation is of the teachers who, as Mary Willes describes, through their 'intonation, gestures and expression' give out 'clues' which the child is left to guess and test the meaning.

The rules and routines are frequently non-negotiable. They are the prerogative of the teacher, which often she does not choose to or think to divulge. Thus, becoming a pupil is seen by Willes as learning these teacher initiatives as rapidly as possible:

> The minimal, inescapable requirement that a child must meet if he is to function as a participating pupil is not very extensive. It is necessary to accept adult direction, to know that you say nothing at all unless the teacher indicates that you may, to know

that when your turn is indicated you must use whatever clues you can find, and make the best guess you can. There are prerequisites to learning this. It is necessary to want adult attention and approval, and to be able to attend to a person or to a topic for more than a moment or two.

(Willes 1983: 83)

This is 'training' in the true sense of the word. It is learning to respond in a given way to a given signal – behaviour with Pavlovian overtones.

Pleasing adults

The notion of pleasing adults is a very important one in the discussion about power and control in classrooms. Holt (1982: 70) suggests that 'it is only when pleasing adults becomes important that the sharp line between success and failure appears'. This implies that children's perceptions of their own success or failure, their own worth and value come from the values and perceptions of the teacher. We know that there is evidence of a self-fulfilling prophecy which operates in classrooms. Tell a child that they are good, will succeed, are doing well and the child obliges by responding with enthusiasm and proving you right. Tell a child that they are worthless, useless, hopeless or any other damning adjective directed at a certain group of children daily in their school lives, and lo and behold they prove you right again. Holt suggests that being incompetent has two advantages: first, it reduces what others expect of you and, second, it reduces what you expect or even hope of yourself. When you set out to fail, he says, one thing is certain, you cannot be disappointed.

Chapter 1 showed that, whatever their experiences, most young children arrive at school as enthusiastic and energetic learners. Their early experience at school can bring about a transformation in their attitudes and behaviours so that they become a shadow of their former competent selves. Such are the expectations of schooling that being a pupil for some children can mean doing what the teacher says and conforming to what the school demands. Howard Gardner (1993: 2), in his powerful book *The Unschooled Mind* suggests that somehow 'the natural, universal, or intuitive learning that takes place in one's home or immediate surroundings during the first years of life seems of an entirely different order from the school learning that is now required throughout the literate world'. In similar vein, Janet Meighan (1993: 43) suggests that once children begin school, 'Learning how to learn gives way to learning how to be taught'.

So we return to the main question of this book: Why, when children in their early, formative years have achieved what Gardner (1993) calls a 'breathtaking array of competences with little formal tutelage', do some of those same children suddenly become dependent, passive learners, reliant on the teacher for success and self-esteem? Gardner (1993: 3) suggests that 'schools were instituted precisely to inculcate those skills and conceptions that, whilst desirable, are not so readily and naturally learned as (their) intuitive capacities'. There is more than an element of truth in this. Schools are devices of society and, therefore, must respond to the requirements of that society and of the cultures it serves. Unfortunately, in fulfilling this requirement, schooling can denude children of all their inherent powers as learners and make them feel as though their needs and their interests are no longer respected. For some children, the transition from home to school marks a transition from success as a learner to failure. All too often it is the child who is a truly intuitive learner who is at greatest risk. Schools do not often cater for individuals. Because of their very nature they demand a good deal of conformity, and schools which are not sufficiently flexible to allow for the idiosyncrasies of learners are likely to alienate some of the most creative and free-thinking children.

Disaffected learners

Feelings of alienation come about when there is a mismatch between the child's expectations of the school and the school's expectations of the child. According to Willes (1983), some pupils apparently 'step out of line' because they do not know where the line is drawn. But some children know where the line is drawn and deliberately cross it. In the introduction to her book on disaffection in the early years, Gill Barrett (1989: xiv) defines disaffection thus:

> Fundamentally the word implies a negative state of something that was once positive. Thus affection for something has been reversed to become disaffection. Here we are concerned with disaffection in the early years of schooling. Thus, instead of affection for the activities of schooling, disaffection implies a dislike and hence a turning away from the activities and learning expectations of the classroom and school.

If one considers that some children will have only just started school, the implication of this definition is that the 'affection' is for learning which takes place in contexts prior to and outside school. Disaffection, therefore, comes hard on the heels of affection for tasks at which children had seen themselves as competent. Running right through this book is the notion of young children as both competent and motivated learners, and it is a dreadful indictment that schools can turn that motivation and competence so quickly into disaffection.

The need to be seen as a learner

We have seen how important it is for children's existing competences and their previous experiences to be viewed as valuable and of intrinsic importance to any future learning and development. Children who have strong feelings of self-worth, the basis for most successful learning, are those who know their contribution to be welcomed and their experiences to be valued. Neville Jones (1989: xii), in his preface to Gill Barrett's book, suggests that, 'By definition, disaffected pupils invariably feel in some respect devalued persons'. When self-esteem is eroded, then children begin to exhibit the kinds of behaviours which show alienation towards the culture of school and the expectations of the classroom. In an occasional paper written for the Council for Educational Technology, Davies (1987) explored different views of what learner autonomy might mean, both in theory and practice. He suggested that it is essential that learners are confident in being able to handle the learning they perceive they need, otherwise they become confused and frustrated, and disillusionment creeps in. He offers evidence that when adults were invited to initiate learning, their learning needs were rarely what had been anticipated. Even their starting points and learning sequence for a given piece of work often differed widely from what the tutor considered logical. If this is true for adults and their tutors, then how much more relevant is it to children and their teachers?

Disaffection in older children

When children are older, they behave in ways that 'have a tendency to exacerbate their feelings of disaffection' (Jones 1989). So with children, particularly of secondary age, we may see disruption, vandalism, maladjustment, absenteeism and truancy. These 'active' forms of behaviour cause many problems for teachers while pupils are in school. But there is another form of disaffection, the passive form, which is 'possibly more insidious'. Pupils simply opt out of ordinary school activities, but in ways the teacher does not always notice. This disaffection can have implications beyond school life and 'maybe throughout the life of the pupil'.

Disaffection in young children

Younger children are much less likely to turn to the kind of active behaviours described above, so how does their disaffection manifest itself when they have feelings of low-esteem and frustration? They are unlikely to withdraw themselves from the environment, as most young children choose to remain within the security of the school even when feeling very aggrieved. Their most likely response is to reject or withdraw from the activities or tasks they are being required to perform. If this withdrawal is 'active' the children can throw tantrums, disappear under tables or absent themselves into another room of the school. Barrett (1989: 30) claims that:

> school, with all its new expectations and people, is likely to provoke strong responses such as crying, hitting other children and removing oneself from the source of frustration. If the child knows that these strong responses have always been responded to by an adult in the past, and the cause of frustration removed and dealt with, then it may cause even stronger response behaviour in school when the initial crying or attempted withdrawal fails to remove the expectation.

If the rebellion is more 'passive', then children simply stop doing what is asked of them, do it extremely slowly or make sure they disrupt as many other children as possible in the process.

There can be no doubt that disaffection arises because children are asked to do things at school which make little sense to them. It is no justification to say that children have to learn to do this in life and, therefore, they should start now. This rationale is used for an astonishing range of experiences, from sitting still during registration to enduring competition in games. Children may have to face a myriad of unpleasant and unhappy experiences before they grow old and die, but this is no justification for inflicting such experiences on children just so they can practise their future unhappiness.

One of the greatest frustrations for young children is that often they cannot articulate their own feelings. They find it hard to explain or describe what they feel and why. Gill Barrett's important study showed that if teachers are patient enough to ask (and willing to find out the answers) why children are not responding positively, then they are half way to resolving the problem for the child and, of course, for themselves and the rest of the class.

A further frustration for young children is the number of times teachers interrupt them when they are engaged in activities. We have seen that one important principle of early childhood education is that the young learner has time for periods of sustained activity. Whether this is initiated by the child or the teacher, an adherence to the principle is crucial if children's experiences of learning at school are to emulate their experiences at home and if the teacher is to communicate positive messages about the worth of the activity in which the child is engaged. Barrett (1989: 10) provides examples of the intense frustration young children feel when their experiences are interrupted:

> Daniel and Carl have found a book on New Zealand (Carl's homeland). They start to read when the teacher calls, 'Time to put them away'. Daniel's face and comment show disappointment. 'But I've only just got it.'

> There are always too many people in school to take things properly. You have to stop too soon. Someone always spoils it.

Many teachers and whole school staffs are addressing the issue of interruptions to the school day. Research by Campbell and Neill (1990) has confirmed what all teachers know, that there is insufficient time in the school day for all that has to be done. But an audit of how time is spent in school can reveal how much learning time is fragmented by the school 'timetable'. Assemblies, playtimes, lunches, television and so on, all interrupt the flow of learning for children. Each break requires teachers and children to wind themselves down and then to wind themselves back up again to achieve the previous momentum. This is not an efficient use of time and it is a useful exercise to examine the interruptions in a classroom or within the school, and see if there are ways in which such interruptions can be minimized (see, for example, the discussion about playtime in Chapter 7).

The negotiated classroom

School, as we have seen, is a place where rules and expectations are frequently governed by adults and where children are unable to stake a claim. It is usually adults who create the learning environment for children, but what happens if teachers consciously and deliberately give children a stake in the process? What is possible if, in order to maintain and sustain their motivation, application and *rights*, children are taken on as partners in the shared negotiation of practice and behaviour?

The notion of negotiation

Sylvia Warham (1993) suggests that in some ways teaching and learning are, in themselves, a negotiation because 'the process requires the consent of both the teacher and the learner'. The negotiation of the learning context between the teacher and the children is a negotiation of what the children will allow the teacher to do and what the teacher will allow the children to do. Successful negotiation requires messages to emanate from the teacher. When children are listened to and their ideas and interests absorbed into the fabric of their curriculum experiences, then this is a positive starting point for the negotiation of the more complex elements of classroom life.

Teacher identity

There are a range of classroom issues which can be negotiated with children. The extent to which these are adopted in classrooms depends very much on the style of the teacher and her personal identity. Warham (1993) identified teachers who had 'dominant identities' and those who had 'less dominant identities'. She suggested that teachers who had dominant identities in the classroom situation 'created inequality. The children found that only one person at a time could be dominant and they had to compete with one another and the teacher if they wanted to take part in the (class) discussion' (pp. 35–6). On the other hand, the less dominant teachers appeared to have 'no control over the situation', but used a far greater range of strategies in interaction with the children than the dominant teachers. By encouraging children to be independent thinkers and learners, the control which less dominant teachers exercise is far more subtle, but far more effective. According to Warham, effective teachers adopt both dominant and less dominant strategies in different situations, but she warned that it is important to be conscious of the positive effects of habitually less dominant strategies which, she claimed:

- foster trust, confidence and security;
- encourage in children a sense of self-worth and respect for others;
- encourage independence and self-reliance;
- encourage children to develop their own initiatives; and
- foster a sense of equality (p. 37).

While habitually dominant power strategies may not prevent children from learning, it is possible they carry with them certain inherent risks. Warham (1993: 37) suggests that it is possible they may:

- foster competition to the point of confrontation;
- damage group and individual relationships;
- discourage the children from taking initiatives;
- make the children dependent upon their teacher; and
- risk damaging the child's future attitude towards teachers and education.

The notion of negotiation can only sit comfortably with the less dominant teacher strategies described above. The remainder of this chapter is devoted to looking at ways in which teachers can move towards the kind of classroom which acknowledges children's competences, respects their rights as individuals and sees education as a collaborative venture between learners.

The possibilities for negotiation within classrooms fall into three broad categories:

- *Organization*: when and how it is to be learnt.
- *Context:* where and with whom it is to be learnt.
- *Curriculum*: what is to be learnt.

Organization

The start of the day

At the beginning of the day, children are full of energy and, we hope, enthusiasm. If they arrive at school and are required to sit down, sit still and (probably) sit quietly, then immediately they are having to adopt behaviours which suit the purposes of the teacher rather than themselves. The children's needs are subsumed beneath the needs of the teacher to sort out the early morning problems, to juggle children and parents, and to be seen as having a calm, controlled class. The beginning of the day does indeed establish the tone for much that will follow. If the day begins in ways which repress children, for whatever purposes, then it sends negative messages to children about those in power and control in the classroom, and in some children can set up feelings of frustration, alienation and resentment before the day has hardly begun.

In some classrooms, on arrival at school, children get straight down to activities which they choose themselves. Parents are encouraged to stay for as long as they can or want, and while children are engaged independently or with their parents or carers, the teacher can get on with her administration or organization in the knowledge that the children are working purposefully. Some teachers are concerned about starting the day in this way because of their responsibilities regarding completion of the register. However, completion of the register does not rely on children sitting on the carpet and responding to their names. In nurseries, children rarely meet on the carpet for registration and yet nursery teachers also need to know how many children are in school at any time. Nurseries have a whole range of strategies for recording the arrival of children, from hanging names on a 'tree' to posting names in a letter box. In some classes, children write their names on a blackboard or whiteboard when they arrive. There are a variety of strategies which teachers can employ if they feel that a formal registration does not set the tone they want for the start of the day.

The organization of the room

When I was in my first year of teaching, I used to spend days before the beginning of each term organizing my classroom. I made labels, signs and charts, spent a fortune on card and pens and tacky-backed *everything*. I believed that it was part of my professional responsibility to make the room as 'ready' for the children as I could, so that it would look a purposeful and welcoming environment in which we could all get down to work. But, as I began to give more time and thought to the involvement of the children in decision-making processes within the classroom, I realized just what wonderful learning opportunities I was taking out of the hands of the children. Real-life problem-solving situations frequently stare us in the face in classrooms, and instead of responding to them as heaven-sent opportunities, we subject children to the contortions of 'identifying a need' for a problem for which they will rarely realize a solution and which they would never in a million years have identified for themselves.

But classrooms *need* organizing. As Chapter 5 describes, there are decisions about space and resources which are fundamental to the establishment of an environment which is conducive to independent learning. Since this is an environment in which children are to learn, then it seems entirely logical that it should be an environment which they help to create. Once I realized this I left the furniture where the caretaker had left it – in a heap in the middle of the classroom (yes, that really *was* his practice!). Then, when the children arrived, we worked together to decide what learning areas were needed and where resources should go. Then came the business of sorting, locating and labelling resources which, because the children were so involved, gave them a sense of ownership over the classroom which they never had when the decisions and the action had been taken by me, when they were not around.

Discipline: rules and sanctions

One successful way of helping children to respect and adhere to rules and sanctions is not to impose them from on high, but to negotiate them. Children can become involved in establishing rules which they perceive to be necessary in order for their classroom to run smoothly and for the benefit of all. Children's rules sometimes reveal interesting insights into their perceptions of what is or is not important and what is or is not likely to happen in classrooms. 'The children mustn't spit' said one 4-year-old recently arrived at school – now where did *that* idea come from?

The sanctions that children work out for themselves can be very enlightening. I had endeavoured, as a headteacher, to alter my role within the school in the disciplining of children. Rather than seeing children only when they had been naughty, I asked the staff to send me children with whom I could share something positive and worthwhile. This seemed to be working well, so I was dismayed when the reception class, on negotiating their own sanctions, ended a long list of mounting retribution with 'No.6. Send them to Miss Fisher for telling off'. Children's perceptions are not altered overnight.

If rules make sense to children and if sanctions seem appropriate, even if not necessarily 'fair' in adult terms, then children are more likely to feel a sense of responsibility in maintaining them. It is also highly desirable that classroom rules do not apply only to children. If the climate of negotiation is to be fostered genuinely then it is appropriate that teachers make a commitment to children about their behaviour also.

One last word about rules – it is best to keep them positive. It contributes so much more constructively to the ethos of the classroom if the list talks about what we *will* do, and be like, rather than what we must *not* do or be like.

Order of work

Negotiation of the order in which children do their work is bound up with decisions about the amount of control we believe children should have over their learning experiences. Chapter 9 sets out various ways of encouraging children to be independent in their movement from one activity to the next. Inherent in this independence is the control that comes with being able to organize work in the order in which it suits the child. Chapter 2 notes that children are 'larks' and 'owls' in the same way as adults are, and if we are to get the best from children then they must be allowed to plan the ebb and flow of their working day as it suits them.

Letting children negotiate the order of their work presupposes an element of trust between teacher and child that work will be completed (see Chapter 9). But this is all part of the negotiation process. If children know that they are being trusted and are being given the opportunity to make their own choices and decisions, then they also know, because it is a part of the 'negotiation' made explicit by the teacher, that they have to fulfil their side of the bargain. Negotiation can never be one-sided and a classroom where children do their own thing, but not the teacher's, is not a negotiated classroom. Part of the developing relationship between the teacher and the class must include discussions about what choice and decision-making means, and it includes the responsibility to fulfil all sides of the bargain and to complete the tasks which the teacher initiates as well as the tasks children want to initiate themselves. On the teacher's side, the bargain is that she does not set up so many teacher activities that the time for child-initiated activity is squeezed out. Planning is critical. If time has been allowed for a balance of activities (see Chapters 4 and 9), then it is perfectly appropriate for a teacher to remind a child that there is only x amount of time now in the day/week and there is still y to be completed. Most children, given the self-respect that comes from making their own decisions, respect in turn their teachers and will complete what is outstanding – even if reluctantly at times. In nego-tiated classrooms where children can choose the order in which they do their work there is a purposeful and dynamic atmosphere. It is rare to see the persuasion and coercion which can go on in classrooms where children are required to complete successive tasks set by the teacher with no room for negotiation or using their initiative.

Length of time on work
When children can negotiate the order in which they do their work, then it is implicit that they will be able to determine how long they will spend on a task. Time management is something which many adults could usefully learn, but even young children can develop this skill when given experiences that leave decisions in their hands. Most children learn to pace themselves given sufficient experience of having control over time and their own learning activities.

As we have seen earlier in this chapter, children need sustained periods of time in order to produce work of quality and depth (EYCG 1992). It is up to the teacher to plan for the delicate balance between sufficient time being given to the needs of the child and sufficient time being given to the demands of the external agenda. Some teachers worry about the child who, despite reminders or help with time management, still works all day on a child-initiated activity, for example the sand tray. If there are a lot of interesting and absorbing activities in the classroom, then most children want to experience more than one thing in any one day. However, if a child is genuinely reluc-tant to move and clearly is gaining something valuable from their self-selected activity, then what is this telling us about that child? If teachers see children's behaviour as a learning opportunity for themselves, then this may be a way of reducing the number of confrontations that can dog classroom practice. Children who need to repeat experiences may be in need of reassurance of something familiar. They may be feeling unsettled or unwell and simply find that repeating something they know offers them the security they temporarily need. If the behaviour is out of character and continues, then this should alert the teacher to investigate the reasons for the child's behaviour. Forcing children simply leads to alienation: it may bring about a temporary result, but will not enhance the children's attitudes or approaches to learning. As Holt (1982: 265) says, 'If the situations, the materials, the problems before a child do not interest him, his attention will slip off to what does interest him, and no amount of exhortation or threats will bring it back'. Children can be trusted to set their own pace. They will need opportunities from the teacher to manage and organize their time, but as with all elements of independent learning, this is time well spent.

Context

Place of work

Where we work can have a significant bearing on our application to a task. I am sure I am not alone in feeling that I cannot do my own writing unless I am in the relative tranquility of my study, and cannot settle to read the Sunday papers unless I have got my legs up on the sofa and the cat on my lap. Locations can promote or inhibit learning and, as with everything else, what is desirable for one person can be thoroughly undesirable for someone else. If a classroom is designed along the lines of the 'workshop' approach outlined in Chapter 5, then children will already have the freedom to move around the room in order to find resources and use equipment. However, this freedom is fettered if children are then required to go back to a predetermined place to complete the task in hand. If a child truly concentrates best sitting alone, lying on the floor, working with a friend, then the classroom should be arranged so that this can happen. Part of negotiation is being able to justify a decision made (on the part of the teacher as well as the children); therefore, a child who chooses an unusual work location may be required to justify it to his or her peers and the teacher. If the quality of everyone's work is not compromised, then the decision is justified. If work is adversely affected, then the teacher and other children are at liberty to challenge the decision, and suggest a different one.

Sometimes, in classes where children are getting used to their independence, there may be some 'flitting' – that is, children going from place to place without settling for long, or watching other children without actually joining in themselves. This situation is another learning opportunity for the teacher. Children who flit fall generally into two categories. There are those who are unsure of themselves, who need to see the range of what is possible but who do not yet have the confidence to try something for themselves. In this case, flitting is very valuable because it means that the child comes to gain confidence through observations and imitation and almost always joins in once this is achieved. Then there are children who need support in gaining independence. Perhaps they are given little independence at home and are used to having things done for them and need support to make decisions for themselves. In this case, the teacher needs to make it part of her 'teaching' (or perhaps that of the classroom assistant) that the child is helped in small stages to begin to make decisions and to act on their own initiative. One of the most important parts of this is to gain the understanding of parents so that they extend independence to the child's life at home.

With whom to work

Most of us work better when we work alongside people whom we like and whom we trust. One only has to try and separate teacher colleagues at inservice training courses to realize just how strong are our adult feelings of security in people we know! If children are not in fixed groups, then for most of the day they should be able to work alongside those with whom they want to work. If they are working on a task as an individual, then it makes no odds whether they are sitting next to somebody doing a different task. There will be times when the teacher wants certain children to work with others (see Chapter 6). However, for the remainder of the time, young children do not collaborate readily unless they see the need to do so, in which case they organize themselves very effectively. So being able to choose who to work with usually gives children an added sense of motivation. However, there are some exceptions to this. Once again it is part of the negotiation process. If children do not work in cooperative and constructive ways with the person or people whom they have chosen, then the rest of the class and/or the teacher can suggest alternative ways of working.

The curriculum

The topic

In Chapter 3, I expressed certain reservations about topic work, in that it can be hijacked by teachers and have little relevance to the class or individual. If choices of topic are not made too early, then the interests of children can be incorporated. If in the medium and long term the subject concepts, skills and knowledge are identified, then it can be left to the individual teacher and her class as to how these are brought together and integrated. An individual teacher can be given an identical set of concepts and skills as her colleague in the next class, but given her knowledge of the particular needs and interests of her class may choose to plan for and integrate these elements in quite a different way to her colleague. Negotiation with children encourages teachers to consult children as much as possible and to amend their planning to take account of children's opinions.

The key questions within a topic

One very successful way of involving children in the overview of their work is to brainstorm with them all the things that they would like to find out about the topic which they are to follow. By raising questions, children come to see that the work they are doing and will be doing has the express purpose of answering these questions. One enter-prising class I know writes their questions on huge bits of card and suspends them from the classroom ceiling so that everyone is reminded that these are the things which are to be investigated. In this way, the teacher is seen as learner alongside the children and the emphasis is on the process of discovery rather than the transmission of facts. When children have ownership of their learning in this way, there are far more opportunities for them to use their initiative both at school and at home to come up with answers or pose more ques-tions of their own.

Criteria for success

One of the ways in which teachers display control in the classroom is by being in charge of what is deemed to be good, appropriate or suf-ficient with regard to children's work. Children come to rely on their teacher's judgements for affirmation and approval and do not believe that their own opinion matters. Teachers use words like 'good', 'well done', 'brilliant' and so on, they draw smiley faces and award stickers. All of these mechanisms say to the child that it is what the teacher thinks that matters here. Judgements about value and worth are by the teacher's criteria. When children are reliant on the teacher's evalu-ations in this way, they are usually left in no uncertain terms about whether the teacher is pleased or not. But very often they can be left quite bemused as to *why* this work was 'fine' and this 'not your best'. In an interesting article entitled 'In praise of praising less', Mark Tomp-kins (1991) warned against empty praise. The article suggests that the teacher should give her *opinion* rather than her *judgement* and make specific reference to the details of the child's activity or the process the child has used. If children have negotiated the purpose of the work and understand why they are doing it, then they are far more likely to be able to give a rationale for when something has been undertaken or achieved to their own satisfaction. In some classes, teachers negotiate with children the 'success criteria' *before* an activity begins. In other words, they ask 'what do you think will make this a successful model plane?', 'what do you think would make this discussion effective?', or 'what will make this an interesting story for the readers in Class 4?' When children are clear about success criteria – where this is appropriate to an activity – then it helps to provide them with a clear framework in which to work.

Audience/use for finished work

Sometimes children are pleased with their efforts and want to share what they have done. Sometimes they are dissatisfied and want to start again. Sometimes they are dissatisfied and want to do something else. If children make a decision that their work is not acceptable to them, then usually they should be at liberty to dispense with it as they choose. Some children screw work up because they are so lacking in self-esteem that they cannot believe they have achieved anything of worth. Whatever the reason for satisfaction or dissatisfaction, choosing what happens to a piece of work should be the child's decision. Yet so often that piece of work automatically becomes the property of the teacher: 'I just want to borrow it for the colour display'; 'you can take it home at the end of term'; 'mummy will be so pleased to see it on the wall'. The 'I just want to borrow this for the wall/portfolio/class book' puts the teacher firmly back in control of what happens to children and their work. There are legitimate reasons for teachers wanting children's work for display. These should be explained to the children. If children then decide to do something for the display in the hall, then that is their choice. If they do not, then that is also their choice and tells us something, perhaps, about the relevance of the hall display to that child.

Planning the day's work

This aspect will be covered in depth in Chapter 9. Suffice it to say here that if children are to have a sense of ownership of their learning and their learning environment, then negotiating their day's work must clearly be part of this. An element of self-selected activity is crucial, not just in terms of motivation but in terms of giving status to a critical element of young children's learning. Children need to be able to negotiate much of what they do, the order in which they do it, the time they spend on it and with whom they do it. The following is a summary of what and when children can negotiate.

The negotiated classroom

Long- and medium-term planning

- Long- and medium-term planning identify the concepts, skills, knowledge and attitudes within each subject that the teacher plans to introduce, revisit, develop over a given period of time.
- The activities identified at this stage should be *possibilities* only.

Short-term planning

- Short-term planning takes account of the needs and interests of a specific class of individuals.
- Teacher-initiated activities and child-initiated activities should occur alongside each other.

The teacher observes and has conversations

- What can the child tell me about themselves as a learner?
- What does each child already know/understand?
- What strategies/skills does each child use?
- How does each child work with others?
- What is the child interested in?

Teacher plans

- What does child need to know now? (concepts/skills/knowledge/attitudes)
- How is this best learnt? (differentiation=activity/process/outcome/grouping, etc.)
- What support does the child need?
- How can I include the spontaneous interests of children? (and who shall give it?)
- Which activity will be teacher-intensive?
- Are the other activities planned so that they can be independent learners?

Child plans

- What work do I want to do today?
- What work do I need to do today?
- In what order shall I do my work?
- Where shall I work?
- With whom shall I work?
- What resources/equipment do I need?
- What do I want to do with my finished work?

- What kind of support/inter-
  vention do the other activities need?
- Have I planned to revise
  both teacher-initiated and
  child-initiated activities?

Teacher observes and has conversations

- Have I planned to observe teacher-intensive, teacher-initiated *and* child-initiated activities?
- Have I planned to involve the child in *self-*assessment?
- What is the focus of my assessment of the teacher-intensive task?
- Will I observe or participate?
- Have I identified the evidence on which to base my assessments?
- What strategies have I established for recording unplanned obser-vations/conversations?
- How will I use all the evidence collected to inform future plan-ning?

Conclusion

If children are to emulate their early success as learners once they start school, then teachers need to ensure that there is not a great gulf between being a child and being a pupil. Children who are expected to behave in ways which are alien and irrelevant to them may become disaffected as learners and this disaffection frequently occurs when children have no control over their own experiences in school. When teachers are committed to a learning partnership with their pupils, then there are many ways in which children can negotiate learning. The power and control this gives children can be a powerful and moti-vating force for learning and is likely to lead to positive, life-long atti-tudes towards learning and accomplishment (Schweinhart *et al.* 1993). Some teachers believe that giving children control means that they themselves will lose it. My experience is that this could not be further from the truth. One reception teacher who evolved a negoti-ated classroom with her children remarked, 'the more control I give away, the more in control I am'. The next chapter draws together the many practical aspects of previous chapters in suggesting how chil-dren can be helped to organize their own learning experiences.

9

PLANNING, DOING AND REVIEWING

Children organizing their learning

Introduction

This chapter looks in practical ways at how young children can organize their own learning. Previous chapters have suggested that in a well-organized classroom, where space is utilized effectively and where children can find and replace their own resources (see Chapter 5), children can work with increasing independence. The role of the teacher is crucial in planning classroom activities which take account of the considerable amount of time which young children spend working alone. The planning of activities needs to acknowledge the difference between the kind of activities which children undertake alongside an adult (teacher-intensive activities) and the kind which are successfully tackled alone (teacher-initiated activities) (Chapter 4). The order in which work is done and those with whom work is done are also features of a negotiated classroom (Chapter 8), and each of these different features contributes towards children's increasing autonomy as learners. This chapter is concerned with how children organize their own learning, how they move independently from one activity to the next and how their independence is supported in constructive and purposeful ways.

There are a number of strategies which teachers use to support children's independence and to encourage their self-discipline and sense of responsibility. One such strategy involves children in having considerable responsibility in planning their own learning in some of the ways described in Chapter 8. This strategy aims to motivate children by giving them opportunities to make choices and decisions in doing their work. It makes explicit their own responsibility in seeing an activity through by including regular opportunities for reviewing and evaluating their achievements.

Planning

> Children who are able to plan for themselves see that they can make things happen. Children begin to view themselves as people who can decide and who can *act* on their own decisions; they have some control over their own activities.
>
> (Hohmann *et al*. 1979: 62)

In classrooms where all the children do the same activity for a pre-scribed period of time, there is little scope for them to plan, because their work and the order in which they do it is dictated by the teacher. However, when teachers plan for a range of tasks to be happening at any one time and children move to the next activity when they have successfully completed the previous one (rather than everyone moving on together), then children have opportunities to have some control over what they do and when they do it.

Children need to plan for both teacher-initiated and child-initiated activities, just as teachers need to provide for both (see Chapter 3). They can decide which activity to begin with and which to do next and so on. Young children may only manage to plan their initial activity. Older children will, in time, be able to plan their whole day (or two days or week). It is important that children know what activities the teacher has initiated and the time-scale for their completion. Some teachers plan a day at a time; some give children two days to complete a set of activities; in some schools even the youngest children are given their tasks for the week and plan their time accordingly.

In order to keep the balance of classroom activities (Chapter 4) and for all activities to have equal status (Chapters 7 and 8), children need to be able to move freely from teacher-initiated to child-initiated experiences. They need to find the ebb and flow of their own day by organizing their time to match their energy levels and interest levels. This does not open the doors to children to play all the time and not work at teacher-initiated tasks. The purpose of negotiation is to accommodate the demands of others and this frequently requires compromise. Children come to understand that part of having the freedom to make choices is the need to accommodate teacher-initiated tasks alongside those which they initiate for themselves. My experience of observing classrooms where children have these oppor-tunities is that the delineation between the teacher's work and their own becomes blurred. Children see all activities as being a relevant part of their school day and work at them with a purpose.

As long as teacher-initiated activities are completed by the time the teacher has specified, then children can start with either a teacher-initiated activity or a child-initiated activity and proceed in any order they choose. In this way, children have a degree of control over their learning and are motivated by the decisions they are able to make. Having this kind of control encourages children to demonstrate growing autonomy as they come to learn that they are accountable for their planning and their action (see Reviewing, p. 139).

Oral planning

In the early stages, planning will be verbal. Children identify what they are going to do and then go and do it. For younger children, the teacher may gather together a range of resources and materials to act as prompts for the variety of activities on offer. This is a good strategy for reminding all children about what is available in the classroom and for drawing their attention to activities or equipment that is not being used regularly.

When children plan verbally, it is necessary for the teacher to record their plans. In this way, the teacher has a record of the range and balance of activities which children choose over a period of time and also a ready reference point for when children review their work later in the day. If a child does not complete the tasks they planned, then this can tell the teacher a lot about the child's level of maturity and whether or not the process of planning and then doing is understood. Being able to *plan*, *do* and then ultimately *review* is a sophisticated process and children need time and support if they are to understand the cycle as a whole.

Recording planning

Once children are able to record their own plans, then there are a number of ways in which these can be represented. Children can draw round an object which is representative of the activity they are going to undertake, draw a freehand picture, draw and write the word, or draw a symbol for the table or area in which they are going to work. The recorded plan helps children to develop their capacity to express their intentions in increasingly complex ways and acts as a personal prompt when children come to reflect on their work later in the day. At every stage it must be down to each child to plan in a way that is useful and relevant for them. The system should be highly flexible and accommodate as many different ways of planning as there are children.

Doing

> Work time is a time for adults to observe and learn what interests children and how they perceive and solve problems, to take cues from children and work along with them and to support, encourage and extend children's ideas.
>
> (Hohmann *et al.* 1979: 72)

To be able to go off and work independently, whether on a teacher-initiated activity or a child-initiated activity, the classroom has to be planned appropriately (see Chapter 5). Young children need constant reminding about where everything is and their responsibility for putting things back when they have finished with them. Children who are used to managing themselves and working independently will be able to settle quickly to their activities. Some will be returning to activities which they have left on the previous day, some will be starting activities which they will initiate and some will begin with tasks which the teacher has initiated.

The order of activities

In classes where children are given the choice to organize their day's work in their own way, they have come up with the following options:

- Doing all the teacher-initiated work first and then initiating their own activities afterwards.
- Doing all the child-initiated work first until reminded by the teacher that the negotiation in this classroom means that the teacher-initiated activities need to be started *very soon* or else time will run out.
- Doing activities alternately, first a teacher-initiated then a child-initiated activity.

Some teachers are concerned that unless they direct the order of work, children will arrive at the same activity or area at the same time, and there will be insufficient space or resources to accommodate them. Such situations are, in fact, a critical part of the problem-solving day for independent learners. Initially the teacher asks 'what do you think you can do about this (problem)?' The children then realize they can go on to another activity and come back to this one later. In time, children will not need to ask the teacher 'what shall I do' but will go through the problem-solving process independently.

Once children are engaged in their independent activities, then the teacher can begin her teacher-intensive tasks and have time and space to work with her chosen group(s) in a focused and profitable way.

Working alongside other children

Chapter 6 discussed the business of grouping and whether and when it is an appropriate strategy to employ with young children. Planning a day which suits children as individuals presupposes that they are not always working in a predetermined group unless they are brought together by the teacher for a teacher-intensive activity or they are working with other children on a collaborative task. Bringing children together to work as a group when they are chiefly working as individuals can cut across the organization of the class. It is difficult for children who are already involved in something to be told to leave it so that they can go and work with particular children on a particular task. This is not likely to bring about instant cooperation. Most teachers who have grappled with this issue have decided that the best solution is to begin group work after there has been a break in the children's work for another reason, such as PE, playtime or assembly.

Interruptions to the school day

This brings me to the number of interruptions in the school day which conspire to stop children from working. Predetermined arrangements such as those mentioned above militate against the sustained periods of concentration which are such an important element in children's learning. People who say that young children have short concentration spans are giving them the wrong things to do. Anyone who regularly observes young children will have seen the total absorption and perseverance they demonstrate when engaged in an activity which interests and challenges them. Such activities can have been initiated by the teacher or by the child. When children rush teacher-initiated activities, it is frequently because they have not understood the purpose of the activity and are completing it for the teacher rather than for themselves.

Once children begin statutory schooling, the interruptions to their day multiply alarmingly. Some of these interruptions are understandable. If there is only one hall between eight classes, then the space needs to be timetabled and everyone needs to keep to their allotted times. But what about playtimes? Why do we insist on children going out to play all at the same time just because it is an established pattern of the school day (see Recreational theory in Chapter 7). Many children have only just settled from assembly or a hall time, or are deeply involved in their activities when they are made to stop and play on demand. Any adult who has control over their own patterns of living, be they work or social, knows that you take a break when you *need* to take a break, when your body tells you that you are ready for a change of scene, or pace or activity. The break is then truly beneficial and gives fresh impetus to the next phase of concentrated activity. This is why a permanent outdoor environment, appropriately resourced and staffed, is the most beneficial answer to this problem. Given such a resource, children can follow the ebb and flow of their work patterns outside as well as in. Children have increased opportunities for using gross motor movement and exercising their bodies energetically. But given that most schools are not fortunate enough to have such a resource for their 4-year-olds, let alone their 7-year-olds, how can this issue be addressed? Most schools have now abolished afternoon playtime. Teachers feel that the disruption to both the working afternoon and the children's behaviour was not conducive to a calm end to the day. But in the morning, playtime is still a feature. In one school I know, the teachers decided that they could be more responsive to the class (if not to individual children) if each class took morning break when that class needed it, rather than all together at a prescribed time. For some classes, on some days, this meant not taking a break at all because the children were absorbed in their work. But for most classes it meant taking a break when the children's concentration and application were on the wane and once the learning opportunities of the session had been optimized. The difficulty with this arrangement is organizing a break for teachers and giving them the opportunity to do all those things that make breaktime so valuable. The logistics of this would need to be worked out by individual staffs and there would need to be universal commitment to the notion of a 'staggered playtime'. However, where schools have good classroom support, it is possible to organize a shift system, as they do in nurseries, to enable each adult to get a break. As playtime is a time when children are often interrupted, in their work and their behaviour, then teachers may want to consider this option.

The role of the adult

The role of the adult in the process of planning, doing and reviewing is critical. As we have seen in Chapters 2 and 6, active learning is a social, interactive process and it is essential that all adults foster a climate which is supportive of this. Chapter 4 examines the role of the teacher in detail, but I like the summary in the new High/Scope handbook, *Educating Young Children* (Hohmann and Weikart 1995), which identifies the effects of a supportive climate on both children and adults:

- children and adults are free to learn
- children gain experience in forming positive relationships

- adults see children's behaviours in terms of development
- children grow in their capacity to trust, be autonomous, take initiative, and feel both empathy and self-confidence. (pp. 50–1)

Hohmann and Weikart (1995: 52) go on to outline five key strategies for creating supportive climates:

- sharing of control between adults and children
- focusing on children's strengths
- forming authentic relationships with children
- making a commitment to supporting children's play
- adopting a problem-solving approach to social conflict.

The role of all the adults in the life of the child are emphasized and the High/Scope approach highlights the necessity of patterns of behaviour being established both at home and school, so that children benefit from the mutual involvement of their families and their teachers. (Further details of the High/Scope approach can be obtained by referring to the handbook.)

Completing tasks: what to do with finished work

In an independent classroom, children need to move from one activity to another without recourse to the teacher. Of course, it would be ideal if every child could have a response to every piece of work immediately. But if we are looking at the realistic use of limited teacher time, then I do not believe this is possible without the teacher's focused work being constantly interrupted. This is another compromise situation and because of the realities of classroom life I would suggest that there are some activities which need an instant response from the teacher and some which just have to wait for one.

If an activity does not require an instant response, what do children do when they have finished the task? If the task is child-initiated, then the child may choose to do one of several things:

- clear away and move on – the process has been more important than the product;
- put the outcome of their endeavours somewhere in the class where it will be safe – a specially located shelf, tray or surface;
- put the outcome somewhere where the teacher and/or other adult will be able to see it when they are ready – perhaps a small table by the teacher's chair;

- take the outcome or the 'story' of the process to the teacher for an instant response.

If the task is teacher-initiated, the child may choose to do any of the following things:

- clear away and move on if the task has been concerned with process and not product (an investigation rather than a problem to be solved);
- put the outcome of their endeavours somewhere in the class where it will be safe – a specially located shelf, tray or surface;
- put the outcome somewhere where the teacher and/or other children will be able to see it when they are ready – perhaps a small table by the teacher's chair;
- take the outcome or the 'story' of the process to the teacher for an instant response.

Whichever they choose, children's independence and their willingness not to interrupt the teacher will rest on their knowledge that the teacher *will* share their work – if they want her to – within a relatively short space of time from its completion. This is one important reason for having a regular review time and we will move on to this a little later in the chapter.

Completing tasks: how do I know they'll do it properly?

One question I am often asked is, if children move from one activity to the next without recourse to the teacher, how do teachers know that they will have done their work 'properly'? There are several issues here. First, teachers know their classes well and very quickly make judgements about those children who usually apply themselves and those who may need a little extra encouragement. Second, when children are engaged in activities in which they have had considerable opportunities for negotiation, their personal commitment and motivation are generally increased. Third, this is where *review time* is so important for teachers. If the teacher and class regularly come together to see and hear about tasks that have been completed, then each child knows that they may be asked to account for time spent on an activity and their own personal efforts and achievements.

What do I do next?

There are many different and ingenious mechanisms which teachers have devised for helping children move independently from one activity to the next. In the nursery environment and, I would advocate, the reception class, children will be predominantly engaged on their own self-initiated activities and there is no need for a system which moves them on. They know the resources that are available, they know how the room is organized, they know how to mix their own paints, sharpen their own pencils and get new paper or books. They are able to sustain their own momentum, moving from one experience to another as and when they are ready.

Although teachers will introduce activities to children when they are together – probably at carpet time – many children will need a reminder of what is expected of them during the day. One way that is successful with many teachers is to supply a list of some kind for children to work from. This list can be just that, a list written on the blackboard or whiteboard, it can be a piece of card in the shape of a 'ladder' with 'rungs' fixed by elastic or Velcro. It can be an individual 'menu', as one student called hers, tailor-made for an individual child or group. Whichever strategy is chosen, a list of some kind is an excellent way of encouraging children to be responsible for their own learning throughout the day.

The type of list, and what is on it, will be determined by the educational philosophy of the teacher. If children are planning their own work, choosing the order of their work and deciding with whom to work, then their work chart will be different from a class of children who are told what to do, when and with whom. The particular strategy which a teacher chooses will be dependent on the extent to which classroom experiences are already negotiated with the children. On the following pages I give some examples of ways in which teachers have introduced lists, charts and 'ladders' to their class. They are representative of classes at many stages of independence, but all of them are reliant on the fact that a teacher has decided to give children some classroom autonomy. Many of them depend on children being given choices and making decisions and many are also dependent on the classroom having the balance of activities outlined in Chapter 4 (teacher-intensive, teacher-initiated and child-initiated activities). You may already be following a model of classroom organization and management which is similar to one of these. If you are, then there may be others which you may feel ready to try out. Or these examples may simply give you ideas which trigger off a composite model of your own. The examples may be used as points for discussion at staff meetings and inservice sessions, and my thanks go to all the innovative teachers who have shared their ideas with me and allowed me to watch them in practice. For ease of reference and comparison, all the examples have been drawn in the same format. I refer to the lists as charts.

Model 1 (from a class of 6–7-year-olds)

- The children are in fixed ability groups.
- Each group has a chart which lists the activities which the children are to do in one day.
- The activities are in the order in which children are to work.
- The activities are a mixture of teacher-initiated and teacher-intensive.
- The teacher works with different groups on the teacher-intensive tasks.
- The charts give children 'free choice' at one specific point in each day.

Issues

- The children are locked into one group, working with the same peers and work is differentiated by presumption not observation (see Chapter 6).
- The children have little independence other than moving from one activity to the next.
- The children do not have opportunities for choosing their own rhythm to their activities (see Chapter 8).
- The children have no opportunity for negotiating space and resources (see Chapter 8).
- Play is relegated to a low status activity (see Chapter 7).

Model 2 (from a class of 6-year-olds)

- The children are in mixed ability groups except when they work with the teacher on teacher-intensive activities
- Each group has its own chart.
- The children do their work in the order on the chart.
- Work on the chart is teacher-initiated, with one identified opportunity for 'choosing'.
- Work on the chart is differentiated mainly by outcome.
- The teacher draws children from these tasks to work on teacher-intensive activities which are differentiated by input.

Model 2 (cont'd)

Issues

- The children are locked into one group, working with the same peers (see Chapter 6).
- The children have little independence other than moving from one activity to the next.
- The children do not have opportunities for choosing their own rhythm to their activities (see Chapter 8).
- The children have no opportunity for negotiating space and resources (see Chapter 8).
- Play is relegated to a low status activity (see Chapter 7).

Model 3 (from a class of 4–5-year-olds)

- The children are in 'home' (mixed ability) groups.
- Each group has its own chart.
- The chart has pictures which correspond with pictures on tables/areas in the classroom.
- Children go to the table as indicated on the chart, where activities are set-out/accessible.
- Activities on the chart are teacher-initiated.
- Children can plan a child-initiated activity each time they complete one that is teacher-initiated.
- The teacher draws children out to work on teacher-intensive tasks which are usually differentiated by input.

Issues

- The children are locked into one group, working with the same peers (see Chapter 6).
- The children have limited opportunities for negotiating space and resources (because of having separate ladders) (see Chapter 8).
- Play is used as a 'carrot' for the completion of teacher tasks (see Chapter 7).

Model 4 (from a class of 4–5-year-olds)

- The children are in mixed ability groups for organizational purposes only.
- There is one chart for the whole class.
- The chart shows the tables/areas where children are to work.
- The activities at these tables/areas are teacher-initiated.
- The children can plan to do child-initiated activities whenever they choose as long as teacher-initiated and teacher-intensive tasks are completed on time.
- The work on the chart must be completed over two days.
- The teacher displays her own chart. This shows her teacher-intensive activities and the children with whom she will be working.
- Children plan the order of their work, bearing in mind whether they will be working with the teacher that day.

Issues

- Difficult to differentiate any teacher-initiated activities by input if all the children are undertaking the same activities.

Model 5 (from a class of 5–6-year-olds)

- The children are in mixed-ability groups.
- Each child has a photo-copied sheet which shows the teacher-initiated activities for one week.
- Children are told at the beginning of the day if they are to work with the teacher on a teacher-intensive task.
- Children can plan child-initiated activities whenever they choose as long as teacher-initiated and teacher-intensive tasks are completed on time.
- Children mark off on their sheet when teacher-initiated tasks have been completed.
- Children record on the back of the sheet all child-initiated activities in which they have engaged.

Issues

- Difficult to differentiate any teacher-initiated activities by input if all the children are undertaking the same activities.

Reviewing

> In the process of recalling what they've done, children attach lan-
> guage to their actions. This makes them more conscious of their
> actions and more able to refer to them and draw upon them for
> later use. Talking about, recalling and representing their actions
> help children evaluate and learn from their experiences. When
> planning and doing are followed by recall, children can build on
> what they've done and learned and remember it for the next time
> they plan an activity.
>
> (Hohmann *et al.* 1979: 88)

Who do children review with?

There are two main opportunities for reviewing work with children.
The first of these is as the teacher has conversations with the child in
the course of the working day, either when she is working with them
on teacher-intensive activities or when she is 'spinning the plates' of
the teacher-initiated or child-initiated tasks. The second is at a time
in the day when a group of children – either a small group or the whole
class – come together with the teacher to review what a number of
children have done.

How many times a day?

Review times are invaluable as times for focusing children's attention
on their work. They are also an opportunity to see who has been doing
what. In both cases they provide ideal opportunities for assessment.
As we shall see in the next chapter, what young children say by way
of explanation or description about the activities in which they have
engaged, reveals so much about their knowledge and understanding
of the task or experience. When children review their work, the
teacher (or the classroom assistant) needs a pencil and record sheet at
the ready. What a child says is hard evidence of the development of
their skills and concepts and is an opportunity that should not be
missed.

It seems that there are two particularly good times in the course of
the day for reviewing work. These are *not* at the end of sessions, a time
when frequently there is a coming together of the class. Rather, it
seems to work better if review times come at the beginning of sessions;
in other words, after playtime and after lunchtime. In this way, not
only does it focus children's minds back on the tasks in hand, but it
can also give fresh inspiration to children as they listen to the ideas
and experiences of others. Of course, the teacher has to make a judge-

ment with the age of the children in mind. There are some for whom this break will not be helpful. But for most children of statutory school age, the beginning of the second and third sessions seems a particularly constructive time to spend on reviewing activities with a small group.

How many children should review at once?

In a class of one teacher and thirty or more children, it would be quite inappropriate to review what every child has done each day. This would be as tedious as register time and most young children would stop listening. From watching teachers experiment with this issue, I would suggest that between five and six children, again depending on their age, would be sufficient. If the teacher has the good fortune to be working regularly with a classroom assistant, then the classroom assistant or parent can take her 'planning' group for review time. Review time should be systematic. It should ensure that all children are *regularly* asked to share their experiences with others and it is recommended that teachers keep a record of the children who review at each session.

What should be reviewed?

Everything! Reviewing should include every aspect of classroom experience. This is *not* the time for only reviewing work done with the teacher or which the teacher initiates. Every aspect of work – teacher-intensive, teacher-initiated and child-initiated – should be reviewed, for all of them should have equal status in the classroom (see Chapter 4). Children are learning through every quality experience they have and the teacher needs to tap into all of these experiences in order to build a rounded profile of the child as a learner.

Conclusion

Young children are capable of an astonishing level of independence if the classroom is organized appropriately and expectations are high. Deciding on strategies for encouraging this independence is something for individual practitioners. Teachers need to be committed to any strategy they adopt (Alexander 1992) and strategies need to be introduced gradually so that children take them in their stride. When children plan, do and review their work, it increases their feelings of involvement in their actions and experiences. There is a far greater chance that motivation will be high and that effort will increase. As with all classroom innovation, children need to see the purpose of classroom organization and should be involved in the evaluation of its effectiveness.

The final chapter examines evaluation and assessment. It is concerned with what teachers need to know about children, about classrooms and about themselves. It asserts that effective evaluation and assessment is critical if curriculum experiences are to be planned which genuinely start from the child.

10

EVALUATION AND ASSESSMENT

What teachers need to know about their children, their classrooms and themselves

Introduction

We have already established that assessment should come at the beginning of the cycle of teaching and learning. In order to plan effectively, teachers need to know what children already know and can do and this is established through rigorous observation-based assessment of children in action and in conversation. However, there is also an important place for assessment at the end of the cycle of teaching and learning, when it is used to evaluate the effectiveness of planning and implementation.

There are three major aspects of classroom life which can be regularly evaluated in order to make changes and adjustments to increase effectiveness: children's learning, classroom organization and the quality of teaching. The three aspects are naturally interwoven, but each should be the focus of evaluation in its own right as well as part of the whole.

The evaluation of children's learning

To evaluate the quality of children's learning, it is necessary to assess what children have achieved, to analyse *how* they learn as well as *what* they learn and to be conscious of their attitudes to learning. Teachers are currently involved in two kinds of assessment which serve different purposes when it comes to evaluating children's learning. *Summative assessment* presents a 'snap shot' of the attainment of a child at any given moment and in pre-selected areas. *Formative assessment* is ongoing and gives teachers evidence of the developing skills and understandings of the children in their class. These two kinds of assessment have different purposes and different processes.

Summative assessment is by definition a summary of achievement. Very often it is required in order to pass on information about a child and, therefore, needs to be brief. In the course of a child's school life, summative information is passed to a number of different people. Parents have a legal right to receive an annual report on their child's progress, including the child's attainment in the National Curriculum if appropriate. The next class teacher or the next school will need a summary of a child's attainment on transfer to help them plan the next stages of schooling. There are long-standing discussions between teachers about how much these records should contain. Teachers writing the reports often feel that a great deal of time is spent on something which is never fully read. Teachers receiving the reports sometimes claim that they do not read them so that they can make their own unbiased judgements about each child and their attitudes and abilities. The fact remains that it is important to have a summary of each child's attainment for those times when progress is not smooth and decisions have to be made about appropriate intervention and support. Summative records of progress, written at regular intervals, can give a good indication of strengths and weaknesses, developmental patterns and gaps in knowledge and understanding, all of which can provide a foundation for the diagnostic assessment of children's current needs.

Formative records serve a different purpose. Rather than being a summary of specific points of achievement in a child's school career, formative records give ongoing information about a child's development and progress. Such records give teachers daily information about what children know and can do and, therefore, provide the necessary information on which to build and adjust short-term plans. As we saw in Chapter 3, short-term plans are concerned with differentiation and in order to plan activities which are appropriate for different children, the teacher has to have detailed knowledge of the children's current learning needs. Formative records provide such information and are the foundation of all good planning. By dint of their concern with the detail of children's development, formative records are often quite lengthy, but these records are not for onward transmission to somebody else. The teacher uses these records either to make decisions about short-term planning or to make judgements about children's attainment for summative purposes. Either way they are personal to the teacher.

The records for these two forms of assessment can be summarized as follows:

Summative records
- brief statements made to summarize information gained through formative records
- frequently in the form of tick-lists or checklists
- a summary of the most vital and relevant information about what the child knows, understands and can do
- usually made at a point of transfer (e.g. on entry, change of class, change of school)
- designed to inform others (e.g. parents, next teacher/school, outside agencies).

Formative records
- ongoing, cumulative records, taken throughout the teaching day
- narrative records of what children do and what children say
- with contributions from parents, children and other adults who work with the child
- providing evidence on which to base future planning
- incorporating analysis and planned action.

Recording formative assessments

Formative assessments are based on the ongoing observations which teachers make of children in action. Recording these is a demanding task, but one which teachers need to make part of their teaching day if they are to plan a curriculum which is relevant and appropriate to the children in their class. Many teachers find it helpful to have a single sheet of paper for each child on which they record date, observation, analysis of learning and action. The *date* ensures that a child's rate of progress is recorded and that each individual spurt or plateau can be seen as part of the child's overall development. The *observation* captures what the child says and does and sets the action in context. This can be written straight on to the record sheet or it can be written on a 'Post-it', which is then transferred to the record sheet. The *learning* analysis uses the teacher's professional judgement to identify the skills, concepts, knowledge and attitudes which the observation represents (see below). This analysis will be done at a later stage than the observation and will be used by the teacher to inform the action column. The *action* column is completed as a result of the analysis by the teacher of the learning needs of an individual child. Completion of this column prompts the teacher to 'fine-tune' her short-term planning and ensures that assessment influences the curriculum. Sometimes, no action is required above and beyond the introduction of the next planned part of the curriculum. At other times, children unexpectedly reveal that they know or do not know something and the teacher needs to adjust her plans accordingly. When summative records are written, they frequently draw on these detailed, ongoing notes and, therefore, the quality of summative records is heavily dependent on the quality of formative assessment strategies.

Skills, concepts, knowledge and attitudes

The key to successful assessment is to be very clear about the purpose of the activity which is being assessed. When teachers plan an activity for the classroom, it is usually as a result of the identification of the learning needs of an individual, a group or the class as a whole. The learning needs are expressed as skills to be learnt, concepts to be

---

Example 7: Focused teaching and assessment 1

A student teacher had planned that a group of children should bake cakes. Her lesson plan identified the following intended learning outcomes:

1 The children will understand more fully the concept of change.
2 The children will use the scientific skills of observing, hypothesizing, predicting and investigating.
3 The children will record their findings in ways which are relevant to them in order to report back to their peers.

The lesson was well planned and the children became engrossed in their task. The student asked open-ended questions and answered the questions which the children raised. In her profiles, however, the student did not record the achievement of the children in relation to the intended learning outcomes of the lesson. Instead, she recorded the children's success in relation to the quality of the cakes that they had made. While this was important for those tasting the cakes, it was not the purpose of the lesson and the information recorded was of little value when the student came to plan the children's next scientific experience.

Example 8: Focused teaching and assessment 2

A group of 4-year-olds were to design their own Christmas wrapping paper. The purpose of the activity was for the children to use pattern in their design. The adult had brought into the class a variety of designs to be used as a stimulus for the children so that they could see different patterns. Following a look at this wrapping paper, it was put to one side and the children began to print their own paper. From that moment on, the support of the adult lost its focus. Rather than reminding the children about pattern and showing the purchased wrapping paper as a reminder, the adult prompted the children to use more of this colour or that shape, to fill in the spaces and to press harder to get a clearer print. In other words, the adult had become more concerned with artistic rather than mathematical achievements and the potential for reinforcing a key mathematical concept (the purpose of the activity) was lost. When making assessments of that session, the adult focused on the quality of the printing rather than the children's understanding and application of pattern.

Example 9: Focused teaching and assessment 3

A class of 8-year-olds were investigating an accident. It was part of their curriculum for history and their teacher had planned that they come to understand the importance of evidence in making judgements about what had happened in the past. Each group had an envelope of 'evidence' about the accident, and had to make a collaborative decision about whether the victim had had an accident or whether foul play was involved. The evidence came from the contents of the wallet of the dead man and the group had to piece together the events leading up to the accident. Throughout the discussions, the teacher went from group to group listening to the children's arguments and reminding them of the task in hand. It would have been easy for the teacher to have concentrated on the discussion itself, ensuring that all took part and that the children listened to each other and so on. This she did, but first and foremost she reminded the children about the necessity for the evidence to be secure. She challenged their reasoning and asked for corroborative proof, she kept focused on the historical skills and concepts which were the purpose of the lesson. When, finally, she and the class evaluated the conclusions they had reached, the children were able to talk in terms of effective or ineffective use of evidence and, because the purpose of the lesson had been so carefully sustained, assessments of the children's historical skills and understanding were easily made.

---

understood, knowledge to be acquired and attitudes to be adopted (see Chapter 2). These are the objectives of the activity and should drive all decisions about which activity is best planned to bring the intended learning about. When teachers begin the planning of activities with these intended learning outcomes clearly identified, then the focus of teaching is easier to sustain and the assessment of children's achievements is more easily targeted.

Assessment and the National Curriculum

It is a legal requirement that children are tested at the age of 7+ and that their level of attainment is reported. This assessment is a combination of standardized tests administered to all 7-year-olds (SATs) and Teacher Assessment (TA). Because of its standardized format, National Curriculum testing produces data whereby one child in a class can be compared to another and a set of children in one school can be compared to a set of children in another. Currently, the proposed 'league table' of results at age 7 has not materialized, but right from its inception there has been universal concern over the inappropriateness of subjecting children as young as 7 to any formal kind of testing (Campbell *et al.* 1993; Cox and Sanders 1994). The purpose of national testing is inherently more political than it is educational (Blenkin and Kelly 1994), for it furnishes those who want it with ammunition for proving or disproving their current manifesto on the state of the country's education system. The kind of assessment which collects summative data can be extremely attractive in terms of reducing the complexities of knowledge and understanding to a single figure or score, easily compared with others in a column of figures. The National Curriculum tests are there, claim Gipps and Stobart (1993), to see that the curriculum is taught. They are a mechanism for checking and for overseeing the effectiveness of *teaching*. They are not concerned with the effects of learning, as they do no more than summarize what a child does or does not know of the limited and subjective range of things they have been asked. Kimberley (1990) suggests that this form of assessment 'leaves no room for manoeuvre – you either achieve a target or level, or you don't'. Even the new level descriptions in the revised National Curriculum for 5–11-year-olds (DFE 1995) are an attempt to *summarize* a child's attainment at the end of a Key Stage. They are intended as a description which best fits the child's performance at a certain point in their school career. In terms of the age range of this book (4–8 years), this summary happens only once (i.e. at age 7) and, therefore, provides only a very limited view of the young child as a learner.

The work of Caroline Gipps and her colleagues strongly challenges the validity of any tests in measuring standards, let alone in raising them. However, the information that standardized tests give can be useful when used alongside other, more rigorous forms of assessment. National Curriculum testing may be time-consuming, but it is not professionally rigorous. The professional demands on teachers to complete National Curriculum tests are not as great as the demands of recording formative assessments, where knowledge of young children and their development are essential prerequisites for making sound professional judgements.

Baseline assessment

Having expressed concern about the inappropriateness of making judgements about the attainment of children as young as 7-years-old, we are now facing the prospect of national requirements to make similar judgements of children on entry to school. As this book goes to press, the School Curriculum and Assessment Authority (SCAA) is preparing a consultation document which will be used as the basis for discussion about baseline assessment before recommendations are made to the Secretary of State for Education and Employment early in 1997.

There has been growing pressure to formalize the information which most teachers begin to gather about children when they first come to school. Historically, this information has been used to make a smooth transition from home to school and to help the teacher establish an appropriate curriculum to meet each child's developmental needs. More recently there have been calls for assessment which establishes the performance of children on entry to school in order that some judgements can be made in the future about the effectiveness of the school in terms of teaching and learning. As with all forms of assessment, the purpose behind baseline assessment has a profound effect on the nature of the procedures selected (Gipps and Stobart 1993; Burgess-Macey 1994). If the purpose of assessment is to diagnose the needs of individual children, then the methods chosen may well be different from those selected if the purpose is to make criterion-referenced judgements about one cohort of children in order for the school to put into context the results of externally imposed national tests which will occur at some future point in the child's schooling. Concern with accountability is putting stress on some headteachers and governing bodies to prove that children have made progress even if, as Rosemary Segebarth writes in the introduction to the OMEP(UK) report on baseline assessment (Wolfendale 1993), 'they appeared at 7 to be "failures" in some imposed tests'.

Once assessments are used to make comparisons between schools then, claim Blatchford and Cline (1992), there are strong motives for trying to develop the notion of 'value-added' at the school entry stage. The notion of 'value-added' assessment recognizes that children's levels of attainment at the end of a particular stage of education are closely associated with their levels of attainment when they started. Value-added assessment acknowledges this by measuring the *progress* which children make whilst at a school rather than simply measuring *attainment*. Measuring progress from one point in time to another can help to highlight whether there are differences in the rate of progress made by different groups of children. This is particularly important in terms of equal opportunities, where differences in ability, ethnicity, culture and gender can have a strong influence on children's achievement. The use of value-added measures alongside contextual factors is potentially a useful way of analysing the effectiveness of schools working in very different circumstances.

However, no form of standardized assessment can take account of individual children. Standardized assessment is usually concerned with limited aspects of children's learning and, as Mary Jane Drummond (1993: 86) argues:

> Teachers are here being invited to reduce the complexity of each pupil's individuality, and the richness of each child's learning, to a meaningless numerical scale. There is no underpinning representation of the process of learning; as a result there is no possibility of using the schedule to understand a child's learning.

There is no reason why such assessment should not form a small part of a wider assessment process based mainly on descriptive techniques designed to capture the complexity of individual learning. However, there is widespread concern that many standardized assessment practices are designed to see young children's learning as deficient (Dowling 1995) and that data from standardized assessment is used to label children and to make inappropriate judgements about their ability and potential.

In their consultation documentation, SCAA usefully summarize the two main purposes of baseline assessment (SCAA 1996). The first, they suggest, is to provide formative and diagnostic information about individual children to the teacher. To achieve this, the assessment should:

- identify the child's strengths and learning needs;
- enable the teacher to plan an appropriate curriculum and match the teaching and learning activities to the child's needs;
- identify the child's individual learning needs including special educational needs; and

- provide information that will inform discussion with parents about their child's learning and progress.

The second purpose is to measure the knowledge and skills of the whole cohort of children entering school, so that future progress can be identified and monitored. This, suggests SCAA, provides schools and LEAs with management information which will:

- assist with curriculum and resource planning;
- form part of a 'value-added' measure; and
- aid accountability

Having identified two such different purposes it has proved difficult at both local and national level to develop a baseline assessment scheme which addresses both at once. Until the purpose is clarified it is impossible to make decisions about when the 'baseline' is to be established. If there is to be an entry profile which is to be ongoing and used to identify children's learning needs then it can begin whenever the child starts school, be that at 3-, 4- or 5-years-old. If, however, it is to become the starting point of a value-added measure, then it has to occur, as near as possible, at the same chronological point for all children.

There is also the issue of what is to be assessed. If the purpose is profiling, then this assessment should reflect the richness and breadth of children's learning. In other words, it should address the affective, cognitive, physical, creative, social and moral elements of each child's development. If it is a 'value-added' instrument, then it may well rely on checklists which, by their very nature, limit what is assessed.

It seems that two kinds of assessment may be required when children start school. The first will be the establishment of a profile of each child's development and progress – as is current good practice. This will draw, at the very least, on SCAA's *Desirable Outcomes for Children's Learning on Entering Compulsory Education* (1996) but will be informed and extended by reference to other documentation which addresses the early years curriculum in different ways, such as local authority curriculum guidelines (e.g. Oxfordshire Early Years Team 1996); the High/Scope Key Experience's (Hohmann and Weikart 1995); and the Foundations of Early Learning from the 'Quality in Diversity' Project directed by Vicky Hurst on behalf of the Early Childhood Education Forum (currently in draft form). Such a profile would:

- be a record of a child's significant learning and progress;
- draw on the knowledge and expertise of parents/carers;
- rely on observations made in the course of the teaching day;
- be recorded in narrative form and dated;
- be used to inform future planning.

The second form of baseline assessment would be used to compare children's achievement on entry with that attained in National Curriculum tests at 7. It would:

- record attainments which are directly comparable with National Curriculum attainments;
- be based on observations made in the course of the teaching day;
- be recorded in a form which could be easily translated into numerical scores;
- allow educators to make comparisons within and between cohorts of children.

Having drawn attention to those aspects of baseline assessment which will be of concern to early years practitioners, there is one piece of evidence from current standardized assessment data which is of importance to all those involved in decision-making about this phase of education. Gill Harper-Jones's (1995) analysis of baseline assessment data from two local education authorities – Wandsworth and Birmingham – has revealed the beneficial effect of nursery education on pupils' performance, which is particularly marked for children whose first language is not English or who come from disadvantaged backgrounds. Evidence such as this is to be welcomed by all those who are fighting to preserve high quality nursery education at the heart of pre-school provision in this country.

Assessment in the early years

Mary Jane Drummond (1993) effectively summarizes early years assessment practices as *seeing* children's learning, *understanding* it and then *putting* our understanding to good use. It is important to examine the key elements of assessment in the early years in order to ensure that practice is once again rooted in principle. The following definitions of assessment draw on Vicky Hurst and Margaret Lally's (1992) chapter in a book devoted to the subject of assessment in early childhood education.

1 *It is rooted in developmentally appropriate practice.*
  Children as learners (EYCG 1992) are actively engaged in building their own cognitive jigsaw of experiences. If teachers are to understand what personal models are being constructed, then the assessment they use must be open to evidence of learning from the perspective of the child. Children bring to school their own conceptions and misconceptions (Gilbert and Osborne 1982; Harlen 1985) and these are sometimes far more difficult to change than teachers might imagine (Postlethwaite 1993). However, if teachers

are committed to closely observing what children do and say as the foundations of their assessment practices, then they will have valuable and accurate information on which to base future activities and experiences.

2 *It occurs in contexts with which children are familiar.*

Marion Whitehead (1992) reminds us that there is a considerable body of knowledge which shows that young children's demonstrated knowledge is radically affected by the social and physical constraints of their immediate surroundings (see also Heath 1983; Tizard and Hughes 1984; Wells 1985; Barrett 1989). If a child is assessed in unfamiliar contexts, contexts in which they feel inhibited or insecure, then the results of that assessment will not be a true reflection of what the child knows and can do. If children are set unfamiliar tasks which do not enable them to draw on previous *successful* experience, then they are unlikely to do themselves justice.

3 *It is based on what children can do rather than what they cannot do.*

Tina Bruce's (1987) famous principle of early childhood education has been used and developed in a range of documents about early years practice. It is such an important principle because it gives the process of assessment a particularly positive tone. Rather than adopting the deficit model of testing which seeks to determine what a child *cannot* do, it starts from what the child can do, or can nearly do (Roberts 1995b). The onus, then, is on the teacher to match the curriculum to the child and not to try and fit the child into the curriculum.

4 *It acknowledges that learning is not compartmentalized under subject headings.*

National Curriculum assessment is divided into subjects and different status is awarded to the subjects within it (Whitehead's 'first' and 'second' division subjects). However, observation of young children engaged in developmentally appropriate practice shows how well-planned activities and experiences cut across all boundaries and enable children to draw on a range of cross-curricular knowledge and understanding. Hurst and Lally give a good example (Example 10).

5 *It recognizes that young children learn best from activities which they are motivated to choose for themselves.*

Note the terminology 'motivated to choose'. Sometimes teachers plan the teaching day as though children are only motivated to do what they have selected for themselves, and that usually involves playing. Children frequently have to do what the teacher has initiated before being allowed to 'choose' what they want to do. My experience in classrooms shows quite unequivocally that skilful

Example 10: The cross-curricular nature of learning

When engaged in a cooking activity, the children may gain experience of English (when discussing the processes involved or consulting the recipe), maths (when counting out spoonfuls, comparing sizes, weights, etc.), science (when observing changes or dissolving substances), design and technology (when observing the effects certain tools such as a whisk have on the ingredients), history (when discussing how cake mixture was beaten before we had whisks), geography (when dis-cussing which part of the world certain recipes come from and finding these on a map), personal and social development (when learning about the hygiene aspects of food preparation, and about which foods are most and least healthy), music (when comparing or imitating vocally sounds made by different utensils), physical education (when learning to control whisks, knives, cutters, etc.) and art (when dis-cussing patterns made by different implements, or decorating cakes or biscuits. (Hurst and Lally 1992: 55)

teachers initiate such interesting activities and experiences that children are often every bit as absorbed and involved in them as those they initiate for themselves. Children can and should be moti-vated by the planned curriculum, but this is more likely to happen when they also have ongoing opportunities to engage in activities which they have initiated for themselves. Whatever the balance between teacher-initiated and child-initiated learning, both should be assessed with equal rigour and purpose.

6 *It stresses that children's learning and achievements are affected by the relationships they have formed with their peers and with adults.*
   Children, like adults, achieve most in an atmosphere that gives them confidence and enhances their self-esteem (Dowling 1995; Roberts 1995a). The relationships which form the bedrock of classroom interaction are best developed in an atmosphere of mutual respect and trust. Classrooms in which children have opportunities to be independent and to negotiate their learning experiences provide the best opportunities for that respect and trust between children and between children and their teachers to flourish.

7 *It is informed by all those who know about and are interested in the development of the child.*
   A rounded profile is jointly created by people who see the child in different contexts and in different ways. Parents are children's first educators and their continuing knowledge of their own child gives

valuable insights into their individual needs and interests. Other adults who work with the child, such as childminders, playgroup leaders, speech therapists, health visitors and educational psychologists, all have and make their specialist contributions which should be valued and used.

8 *It is rooted in principles of equality of opportunity and the celebration of diversity.*

Many of the materials used in tests are 'culturally alien' to many bilingual and working-class children (Gipps and Stobart 1993). The revised National Curriculum still does not identify a place for the languages of many bilingual British-born children. Whitehead (1992: 103) suggests that 'by actually naming "English" as a core language component for all schools we lose a crucial perspective on the central role of any human language in cognition and personal and cultural development'. Early years assessment practices recognize individuality and, therefore, diversity. The planning of an appropriate curriculum draws on the current and previous experiences of children, and inevitably includes the distinctive features of their culture and communities. It is crucial that practitioners constantly scrutinize the context and content of their planned activities to ensure that materials are not culturally biased and that they do not portray stereotypical images or militate against the everyday experience or interest of girls as opposed to boys.

Making value judgements

Educational assessment is an 'imprecise activity' (Blenkin and Kelly 1992), in that it must depend to a great extent on judgements and those judgements can never be neutral. We bring to any assessment of children all our own expectations, presumptions, preferences and bias. Of course, just because we cannot make truly neutral judgements does not mean that we abandon the practice altogether; rather, we must become more aware of our own value systems and what we as assessors are likely to bring to any assessment situation. Drummond *et al.* (1992), in their training materials, *Making Assessment Work*, warn that it is all too easy to make judgements based on *assumptions* about what we expect children to do, to think, to feel and to be and not on what children actually do.

Making time for assessment

Chapter 2 explained why observation and conversation are the key strategies on which early years assessments should be based. Both of these require teachers' close attention and it can be difficult in a large class to find the time for either, unless children are encouraged to be independent learners. Chapter 4 suggested ways in which teachers can make time for assessment, but these are all based on the maxim that time must be planned. Assessment is too important to be fitted in when there is a spare moment or attempted when children are demanding attention. While some assessment clearly takes place when an adult is working with a group, this is not sufficient. Many observations require the adult to be independent of children, and this requires children to be able to work independently of adults.

Planning the use of time for assessment

The following is a useful checklist for planning the use of time for formative assessment:

- What evidence is required?
- Is the assessment to find out what children *already* know/can do or what they know/can do *after* a period of teaching?
- Is the evidence best gathered during or after the activity?
- Who will gather the evidence?
- What technique best serves the assessment purpose?
- How and by whom will the evidence be recorded?
- How will the evidence inform future planning?

Gathering evidence of children's learning

What evidence is required?
There is a difference between obtaining information about children's learning and gathering evidence of their learning. We collect *information* about children's learning:

- from previous summative records
- from parent consultations.

These are important but are not sufficient. Information can be dated or open to misinterpretation. Effective planning is based on current *evidence* and is gathered in a variety of ways:

- collecting tangible end-products
- photocopying pictures/writing/mark-making, etc.
- taking photographs
- making audio/video recordings
- observation of what children do
  - the process of learning
  - their learning styles and strategies

  - their knowledge and understanding
  - their skills and attitudes
- recording what children say
  - their developing understandings
  - their misunderstandings
  - their explanations
  - their enthusiasms.

Is the assessment to find out what children already know/can do
or what they know/can do after a period of teaching?
It is important that teachers assess the quality of their teaching particularly in relation to the effectiveness of an activity in bringing about intended learning. However, there is another equally important kind of assessment which seeks evidence of the knowledge and understanding children bring to a learning experience. This is evidence which teachers need before planning rather than after teaching. Both kinds of assessment are necessary and teachers have to make professional judgements about the timing of assessments which have these different purposes.

Is the evidence best gathered during or after the activity?
When there is the opportunity, observation-based assessment gives teachers their best first-hand evidence. There are, however, occasions when observation is neither feasible nor sufficient. When there is only one teacher in a classroom, or even when there are more adults, it is simply not possible to make observations of the learning of more than one individual or small group of children at any one time. Therefore, there are times when teachers need to talk with children after an activity is finished in order to find out what they did and what they now understand. Sometimes, teachers want to give children the opportunity to describe their experiences either to an adult and/or to their peers (see the section on Reviewing in Chapter 9). In this instance, conversations become the key strategy.

Who will gather the evidence, where and when?
Who? (adults)
- the teacher
- another adult.

Who with? (the children)
- child alone
- children working with the teacher
- children working with another adult
- children working without an adult.

Where?
- inside the classroom
- outside the classroom
- in the hall
- in the playground.

When?
- before or after teaching
- while working with child/children
- while child/children working independently.

What technique best serves the assessment purpose?
There are a variety of assessment techniques which all have their value. The decision that teachers have to make is which technique will give them the evidence they need. For excellent descriptions of different techniques and their uses (e.g. time sampling, frequency sampling, audiotaping and targeted observation), see Drummond *et al.* (1992) and Bartholomew and Bruce (1993).

How and by whom will the evidence be recorded?
Certain kinds of evidence 'speaks for itself'. Pieces of writing, photographs, tape recordings and photocopies only need annotation to make them valuable evidence of the stage in a child's development. But the annotation is important, for without it the precise context for learning will be forgotten. Evidence of this kind should be annotated with:

- the name of the child;
- the date;
- the learning context;
- child's comments (if any);
- level of support from adult(s)/other children (if any); and
- National Curriculum level description (if appropriate).

When evidence is based on what a child does or says, then it is up to the adults to record this in a way which is both efficient and effective. The learning materials on assessment prepared by Mary Jane Drummond and her colleagues provide helpful examples of methods of writing down observations and assessments.

Self-assessment

An important element in children's involvement in their own learning is the opportunity they have for self-assessment. When children are engaged in making decisions about what they have done and how they have done it, then it inevitably adds to their self-esteem. If children only ever receive judgements about their work and their achievements from adults, then they will not learn the critical life skill of self-motivation. Here are some questions which teachers believe encourage children to reflect on themselves as learners:

- What interests me?
- What do I enjoy doing?
- What do I want to be able to do?
- What helps me to learn?
- What would I like to know?

The following questions can support a child in reviewing a particular piece of work, an activity or an experience:

- Do I know what I want to achieve?
- Do I think I need help?
- Do I know who/how to go about getting help?
- Have I thought how this might be evaluated?
- How will I evaluate it?

In Chapter 8, we saw how children can be involved in determining the success criteria for an activity. Children have their own and very clear perceptions of classroom and school experiences. It would be an interesting exercise to imagine what the children in your class might answer if they were asked the above questions – then ask them, and see if you were right!

Evaluating classroom organization

Teachers make other observations in classrooms which are not specifically to do with the development of individual children. These are concerned with how smoothly the class runs, how cooperative children are, whether good use is being made of space and resources, and whether the classroom environment is contributing to the quality of children's learning. This information can be gathered in different ways, and here I have identified four possibilities.

Observation of one child
Such observation provides evidence of the organization and planning of experiences:

- Does the child move purposefully from one activity to the next?
- Are there times when the child wastes time, by queuing for example?

- Does the child know how to be independent, or do they frequently turn to other children or adults for support?
- Are the child's experiences positive?
- Are the child's experiences balanced and appropriate?

Observation of one activity
Such observation provides evidence of the responses of different children to the same planned activity:

- How do the children's responses to the activity differ?
- Is the activity successful in meeting the needs of all the children for whom it was planned?
- Are the children learning what was intended?
- If not, does their learning lead the teacher to new understandings about the nature of the activity or the interests of the children?

Observation of the whole class
Such observation is planned to highlight issues of space, resourcing, interaction and independence:

- Is there sufficient space in the classroom for children to engage in active learning?
- Are all the tables and areas in the classroom used effectively, or are some wasting space?
- Are resources easily accessible to the children?
- Do the children responsibly return resources to their appropriate location?
- Do the children interrupt their peers and adults unnecessarily?
- Are the children able to manage themselves independently?

Observation of the teacher
This is perhaps the most challenging but potentially the most enlightening type of observation of all!

- What do I spend my time doing in the classroom?
- Do I spend more time talking than the children?
- Do I listen to the children as well as initiate conversations?
- Do I ask the children questions to which I already know the answer?
- Have I planned activities which interest and engage the children?
- Am I interrupted unnecessarily by the children?
- What strategies am I using to make the children more independent?
- At the end of the day, have I done what I planned to do?

In order to support teachers in carrying out an audit of their current provision and practice, the Oxfordshire Early Years Team (1996) have devised the following prompt sheet. Under each heading there are

An audit of early years provision and practice

1 **An appropriate curriculum**
   i.e. planned to develop the whole child?
   • experiences relevant to child's *current* needs
   • not subject to the National Curriculum (NC) (U5)*
   • planned via areas of learning (U5).

2 **An approach to learning which emphasizes talk and play**
   i.e. planned opportunities for children to talk to each other and to adults
   • children encouraged to initiate conversations and raise questions
   • literacy opportunities in imaginative play areas
   • play observed and assessed
   • opportunities for play *constantly* available.

3 **Periods of time for sustained self-initiated activity**
   i.e. children have the opportunity to make choices and decisions
   • children not interrupted by the 'fixed' timetable (primary assemblies are not compulsory for U5s)
   • constant access to outdoor area for learning ('playtime' unnecessary).

4 **Ample space for play and active learning both indoors and outdoors with due regard for health and safety**
   i.e. DFE guidelines state 2.3 m^2 per child indoors; 9 m^2 outdoors (U5)
   • space created for play activities and active learning (tables and chairs kept to a minimum)
   • an outdoor area planned and organized for learning.

5 **A rich variety of resources for outdoor and indoor experiences**
   i.e. money spent on play resources as well as NC resources
   • sufficient play resources in the classroom
   • a range of age-appropriate resources outside (e.g. bikes, small PE equipment, sand, construction, climbing frame).

6 **An appropriate ratio of adults to children – all the time**
   i.e. DFE guidelines for nurseries is 1:13 (*trained* staff)
   • classroom support is consistent and available the whole day.

* When an indicator is most appropriate for the under-fives, it is shown in parentheses (U5).

---

7 Strong home/school partnerships
i.e. an appropriate induction programme which draws on children's previous experience
- parents involved in contributing to an initial and ongoing profile of their child.

8 Appropriately trained and experienced educators with a knowledge of child development
i.e. teachers appropriately trained for the age/year group
- teachers have acquired further training/qualifications in early childhood education
- other staff have appropriate qualifications for working in early years.

9 Collaborative planning based on systematic observation of children in all areas of development
i.e. systematic observation by *all* adults who work with the child (e.g. teacher, nursery nurse, LSA, parent)
- collaborative planning by all those involved in the observation
- observations feed into formative records which inform planning
- assessments of both teacher-initiated and self-chosen activities.

10 Appropriate facilities
i.e DFE guidelines for nurseries recommend 1 toilet per 10 children, a Belfast sink and hand-held shower facility (U5)
- provision for children to rest during the day if necessary (U5).

---

bullet points which suggest key indicators of quality provision and practice. All of these indicators were taken from recent reports on early years education: the HMI report, *The Education of Children Under Five* (DES 1989), the Rumbold Report, *Starting with Quality* (DES 1990), the report of the National Commission on Education, *Learning to Succeed* (1993) and the report of the RSA, *Start Right: The Importance of Early Learning* (Ball 1994). The consensus within these documents about what constitutes high-quality provision and practice in the early years is overwhelming. It might be useful to share this audit with those who are responsible for and manage schools, to ensure that children in the early years are receiving their entitlement.

The quality of teaching

Reflective practice

> The importance of self-knowledge for the educator is plainly spelled out: effective educators are those whose work includes the study of themselves, their knowledge, their feelings and the frameworks within which they understand children.
>
> (Drummond 1993: 117)

Teachers sometimes spend so long monitoring and assessing the performance of children that they forget that the process is as important for themselves. Yet it is as crucial for teachers to assess themselves as it is for them to assess the children in their class. Being a professional educator requires teachers to be continually developing their own practice and this is not possible unless time is set aside to be reflective and open to change.

The notion of reflective teaching stems from John Dewey (1933), who contrasted 'routine action' with 'reflective action'. According to Dewey, routine action is guided by factors such as tradition and habit and by institutional definitions and expectations. Reflective action, on the other hand, involves a willingness to engage in constant self-appraisal and development. It requires teachers to be flexible and to be willing to analyse rigorously their current practice in order to bring about change. Pollard and Tann (1993: 9) identify six key characteristics of reflective practice:

1 Reflective teaching implies an active concern with aims and consequences, as well as means and technical efficiency.
2 Reflective teaching is applied in a cyclical or spiralling process, in which teachers monitor, evaluate and revise their own practice continuously.
3 Reflective teaching requires competence in methods of classroom enquiry, to support the development of teaching competence.
4 Reflective teaching requires attitudes of open-mindedness, responsibility and wholeheartedness.
5 Reflective teaching is based on teacher judgement, which is informed partly by self-reflection and partly by insights from educational disciplines.
6 Reflective teaching, professional learning and personal fulfilment are enhanced through collaboration and dialogue with colleagues.

Action research

One rigorous way in which many teachers now adopt the process of reflection is through engaging in action research in their own settings.

Action research has two essential aims, to *improve* and to *involve*. The involvement is critical to the practitioner. Instead of research which makes judgements on teachers, teachers are in a position to control what is to be studied and how. Teachers also determine what should be done with any outcomes – are they for their own reflective purposes or could they be used for further study or for sharing with a wider body of colleagues and professionals?

Carr and Kemmis (1986) claimed that action research provides a means of 'becoming critical' and they identified a cyclical model of planning, acting, observing and reflecting which encapsulated Schön's (1987) notion of 'reflection-on-action'. Handal suggested that the normal conditions for school-based action research may well be such that an incomplete 'self-reflective' cycle occurs and teachers spend most of their time planning and acting and less time observing and reflecting (quoted in Day 1993). There has always been a tendency for this to happen in schools, but we have seen that it is reflection and action that are the key ways in which teachers improve their practice. An examination of practice in systematic ways can, of course, challenge existing theories and beliefs. In action research, say Pollard and Tann (1993), practitioners must be prepared to explore the discrepancies between their current practice and the new insights that might be acquired. Whatever methodology is used by teachers, the notion of self-evaluation is every bit as critical for them as it is for children. Reflection should lead to new ways of working (Adelman 1985) and, in order for this to happen, teachers need to be explorers and enquirers in the best traditions of early years practice.

Conclusion

Evaluation and assessment practices are crucial because they can bring about change. Research and experience are constantly informing the dynamic nature of classroom pedagogy and the outcomes of reflection on practice lead teachers to make improvements for both children and themselves. The quality of children's experiences at school are a result of the effectiveness of teachers in evaluating their own performance, as well as the performance of the children, and having the knowledge and skills to translate their evaluations into effective planning and teaching.

Assessment lays the foundations for quality teaching and learning. When teachers watch and listen to children, they put themselves in the role of learner alongside their pupils, finding out what they know and can do. Observation of children in action reveals just what a range of competences young learners have acquired. It reveals how differently young children approach their learning and what a range of needs and interests they have. When teachers get to know children this well, it becomes impossible to fit them all into the same curriculum mould. The competences of young learners demand that teachers respond to children's individual and idiosyncratic learning needs. If the planned curriculum is to be relevant and purposeful then what is taught and learnt in classrooms needs to start from the individual learner – it needs to start from the child.

REFERENCES

Adelman, C. (1985) Action research, in S. Hegarty and P. Evans (eds), *Research Methods in Special Education*. Windsor: NFER.

Adelman, C. (1992) Play as a quest for vocation, *Journal of Curriculum Studies*, 24(2): 139–51.

Alexander, R. (1992) *Policy and Practice in Primary Education*. London: Routledge.

Alexander, R., Rose, J. and Whitehead, C. (1992) *Curriculum Organisation and Classroom Practice in Primary Schools: A Discussion Paper*. London: DES.

Anning, A. (1991) *The First Years at School*. Milton Keynes: Open University Press.

Athey, C. (1990) *Extending Thought in Young Children: A Parent–Teacher Partnership*. London: Paul Chapman.

Aubrey, C. (ed.) (1994) *The Role of Subject Knowledge in the Early Years of Schooling*. London: Falmer Press.

Ball, C. (1994) *Start Right: The Importance of Early Learning*. London: RSA.

Barnes, D. and Todd, F. (1977) *Communication and Learning in Small Groups*. London: Routledge and Kegan Paul.

Barnes, D., Britton, J. and Rosen, H. (1969) *Language, the Learner and the School*. Harmondsworth: Penguin.

Barrett, G. (ed.) (1989) *Disaffection from School? The Early Years*. Lewes: Falmer Press.

Bartholomew, L. and Bruce, T. (1993) *Getting to Know You*. London: Hodder and Stoughton.

Bealing, D. (1972) Organisation of junior school classrooms, *Educational Research*, 14: 231–5.

Bennett, N. and Kell, J. (1989) *A Good Start? Four Year Olds in Infant Schools*. Oxford: Blackwell.

Bennett, N., Desforges, C., Cockburn, A. and Wilkinson, B. (1984) *The Quality of Pupil Learning Experiences*. Hove: Lawrence Erlbaum Associates.

Bennett, S.N., Wragg, E.C., Carre, C.G. and Carter, D.G. (1992) A longitudinal study of primary teachers' perceived competence in, and concerns about, the National Curriculum implementation, *Research Papers in Education*, 7: 53–78.

Bilton, H. (1994) Morning and afternoon sessions in the nursery, do they have equal status? With particular reference to story time, *International Journal of Early Years Education*, 2(2): 54–64.

Blatchford, P. and Cline, T. (1992) Baseline assessment for school entrants, *Research Papers in Education*, 7(3): 247–69.

Blenkin, G.M. and Kelly, A.V. (eds) (1987) *Early Childhood Education: A Developmental Curriculum*. London: Paul Chapman.

Blenkin, G.M. and Kelly, A.V. (eds) (1992) *Assessment in Early Childhood Education*. London: Paul Chapman.

Blenkin, G.M. and Kelly, A.V. (eds) (1994) *The National Curriculum and Early Learning*. London: Paul Chapman.

Boulter, C. (1992) 'Collaborating to investigate questions: A model for primary science', unpublished PhD thesis. University of Reading.

Bradekamp, S. (ed.) (1987) *Developmentally Appropriate Practice in Early Childhood Programs Serving Children from Birth through Age 8*. Washington, DC: NAEYC.

Brierley, J. (1994) *Give Me a Child Until He is Seven*, 2nd edn. London: Falmer Press.

Britton, J. (1970) Speech in the school, *NATE Journal*, Summer, pp. 22–4.

Brown, D. (1994) Play, the playground and the culture of childhood, in J.R. Moyles (ed.), *The Excellence of Play*. Buckingham: Open University Press.

Brown, G. and Wragg, E.C. (1993) *Questioning*. London: Routledge.

Brown, S. and Cleave, S. (1990) *Four Year Olds in School: Meeting Their Needs*. Slough: NFER.

Bruce, T. (1987) *Early Childhood Education*. Sevenoaks: Hodder and Stoughton.

Bruce, T. (1991) *Time to Play in Early Childhood Education*. Sevenoaks: Hodder and Stoughton.

Bruner, J.S. (1966) *Toward a Theory of Instruction*. Cambridge, MA: Harvard University Press.

Bruner, J.S. (1977) Introduction, in B. Tizard and D. Harvey (eds), *The Biology of Play*. London: Spastics International Medical Publications.

Bruner, J.S. (1980) *Under Five in Britain: The Oxford Pre-school Research Project*. Oxford: Grant McIntyre.

Bruner, J.S. (1985) Vygotsky: A historical and conceptual perspective, in J.V. Wertsch (ed.), *Culture, Communication and Cognition: Vygotskian Perspective*. Cambridge: Cambridge University Press.

Bruner, J.S. (1986) *Actual Minds, Possible Worlds*. Cambridge, MA: Harvard University Press.

Bruner, J. and Haste, H. (eds) (1987) *Making Sense: The Child's Construction of the World*. London: Methuen.

Burgess-Macey, C. (1994) Assessing young children's learning, in P. Keel (ed.), *Assessment in the Multi-ethnic Primary Classroom*. Stoke-on-Trent: Trentham.

Calderhead, J. and Miller, E. (1985) The integration of subject matter knowledge in student teachers' classroom practice. Paper presented to the *British Educational Research Association Conference*, Sheffield.

Campbell, R.J. and Neill, S.R.St.J. (1990) *Thirteen Hundred and Thirty Days: Final Report of a Pilot Study of Teacher Time in Key Stage 1, Commissioned by the Assistant Masters and Mistresses Association*. Warwick: University of Warwick Department of Education.

Campbell, R.J., Evans, L., Neill, S.R.St.J. and Packwood, A. (1993) *The Use and Management of Infant Teachers' Time: Some Policy Issue*. Stoke-on-Trent: Trentham.

Carnegie Corporation of New York (1994) *Starting Points: Meeting the Needs of Our Youngest Children*. New York: Carnegie Corporation.

Carr, W. and Kemmis, S. (1986) *Becoming Critical: Education, Knowledge and Action Research*. Lewes: Falmer Press.

Central Advisory Council for Education (CACE) (1967) *Children and their Primary Schools* (The Plowden Report). London: HMSO.

Chang, G.L. and Wells, G. (1988) The literate potential of collaborative talk, in M. Maclure, T. Phillips and A. Wilkinson (eds), *Oracy Matters*. Milton Keynes: Open University Press.

Clarricoates, K. (1983) Classroom interaction, in J. Whyld (ed.), *Sexism in the Secondary Curriculum*. London: Harper and Row.

Cousins, J. (1990) Are your little humpty dumpties floating or sinking?, *Early Years*, **10**(2): 28–38.

Cox, C.B. and Boyson, R. (eds) (1975) *The Fight for Education: Black Paper 1975*. London: Dent.

Cox, C.B. and Boyson, R. (eds) (1977) *Black Paper 1977*. London: Maurice Temple Smith.

Cox, C.B. and Dyson, A.E. (eds) (1969a) *Fight for Education: A Black Paper*. London: Critical Quarterly Society.

Cox, C.B. and Dyson, A.E. (eds) (1969b) *Black Paper Two*. London: Critical Quarterly Society.

Cox, C.B. and Dyson, A.E. (eds) (1970) *Black Paper Three: Goodbye Mr Short*. London: Critical Quarterly Society.

Cox, T. and Sanders, S. (1994) *The Impact of the National Curriculum on the Teaching of Five-year-olds*. London: Falmer Press.

Curtis, A. (1994) Play in different cultures and different childhoods, in J.R. Moyles (ed.), *The Excellence of Play*. Buckingham: Open University Press.

Darling, J. (1994) *Child-centred Education and its Critics*. London: Paul Chapman.

David, T., Curtis, A. and Siraj-Blatchford, I. (1992) *Effective Teaching in the Early Years: Fostering Children's Learning in Nurseries and in Infant Classes*. Stoke-on-Trent: Trentham.

Davies, W.J.K. (1987) *Towards Autonomy in Learning: Process or Product?* London: Council for Educational Technology.

Day, C. (1993) Reflection: A necessary but not sufficient condition for professional development, *British Educational Research Journal*, **19**(1): 83–93.

Department for Education (DFE) (1995) *Key Stages 1 and 2 of the National Curriculum*. London: DFE.

Department of Education and Science (DES) (1989) *The Education of Children Under Five*. London: HMSO.

Department of Education and Science (DES) (1990) *Starting with Quality* (The Rumbold Report). London: HMSO.

Dewey, J. (1933) *How We Think: A Restatement of the Relation of Reflective Thinking to the Educative Process*. Chicago, IL: Henry Regnery.

Dillon, J.T. (1981) To question or not to question during discussion, *Journal of Teacher Education*, **32**(5): 51–5.

Donaldson, M. (1978) *Children's Minds*. London: Fontana.

Dowling, M. (1995) *Starting School at Four: A Joint Endeavour*. London: Paul Chapman.

Drummond, M.J. (1993) *Assessing Children's Learning*. London: David Fulton.

Drummond, M.J., Rouse, D. and Pugh, G. (1992) *Making Assessment Work*. Nottingham: NES Arnold/National Children's Bureau.

Dunn, J. (1988) *The Beginning of Social Understanding*. Oxford: Blackwell.

Early Years Curriculum Group (EYCG) (1992) *First Things First: Educating Young Children*. Oldham: Madeleine Lindley.

Early Years Curriculum Group (EYCG) (1995) *Four-year-olds in School: Myths and Realities*. Oldham: Madeleine Lindley.

Edwards, D. and Mercer, N. (1987) *Common Knowledge: The Development of Understanding in the Classroom*. London: Methuen.

Edwards, V. and Redfern, A. (1988) *At Home in School: Parent Participation in Primary Education*. London: Routledge.

Entwhistle, N. (1987) *Understanding Classroom Learning*. Sevenoaks: Hodder and Stoughton.

Fein, G.G. (1981) Pretend play in childhood: An integrative review, *Child Development*, **52**(4): 1095–1118.

Fisher, J. (1996) Reflecting on the principles of early years practice, *Journal of Teacher Development*, **5**(1): 17–26.

Fisher, R. (1990) *Teaching Children to Think*. Oxford: Blackwell.

Forman, E.A. and Cazden, C.B. (1985) Exploring Vygotskian perspectives in education: The cognitive value of peer interaction, in J.V. Wertsch (ed.), *Culture, Communication and Cognition: Vygotskian Perspective*. Cambridge: Cambridge University Press.

French, P. and Maclure, M. (1983) Teacher questions and pupil answers: An investigation of questions and answers in the infant classroom, in M. Stubbs and H. Hillier (eds), *Readings in Language, Schools and Classrooms*, 2nd edn. London: Methuen.

Galton, M. and Patrick, H. (eds) (1990) *Curriculum Provision in Small Primary Schools*. London: Routledge.

Galton, M. and Williamson, J. (1992) *Group Work and the Primary Classroom*. London: Routledge.

Galton, M., Simon, B. and Croll, P. (1980) *Inside the Primary Classroom*. London: Routledge and Kegan Paul.

Gardner, H. (1993) *The Unschooled Mind: How Children Think and How Schools Should Teach*. London: Fontana.

Garvey, C. (1977) *Play*. London: Fontana.

Gilbert, J.K. and Osborne, R.J. (1982) Studies of pupils' alternative frameworks or misconceptions in science, in W.F. Archenhold *et al.* (eds), *Cognitive Development Research in Science and Mathematics*. Leeds: University of Leeds.

Gipps, C. and Stobart, G. (1993) *Assessment: A Teachers' Guide to Issues*. Sevenoaks: Hodder and Stoughton.

Gura, P. (ed.) (1992) *Exploring Learning: Young Children and Blockplay*. London: Paul Chapman.

Hall, N. (1987) *The Emergence of Literacy*. Sevenoaks: Hodder and Stoughton.

Harlen, W. (ed.) (1985) *Primary Science. Taking the Plunge*. Oxford: Heinemann Educational.

Harper-Jones, G. (1995) Developing baseline assessment: A useful tool or a necessary evil? Paper presented to the *European Early Childhood Education Research Association Conference*, Paris.

Hastings, N. and Schweiso, J. (1995) Tasks and tables: The effects of seating arrangements on task engagement in primary schools, *Educational Research*, **37**(3): 279–91.

Heath, S.R. (1983) *Ways with Words: Language, Life and Work in Communities and Classrooms*. Cambridge: Cambridge University Press.

Hoddinott, B. (1993) Differentiation: Making it work, *RE Today*, Autumn, pp. 42–4.

Hohmann, M. and Weikart, D. (1995) *Educating Young Children*. Ypsilanti, MI: High/Scope Press.

Hohmann, M., Banet, B. and Weikart, D.P. (1979) *Young Children in Action*. Ypsilanti, MI: High/Scope Press.

Holt, J. (1982) *How Children Fail*, 2nd edn. Harmondsworth: Penguin.

Hughes, M. (1986) *Children and Number*. Oxford: Blackwell.

Hurst, V. (1994) Observing play in early childhood, in J.R. Moyles (ed.), *The Excellence of Play*. Buckingham: Open University Press.

Hurst, V. and Lally, M. (1992) Assessment and the nursery curriculum, in G.M. Blenkin and A.V. Kelly (eds), *Assessment in Early Childhood Education*. London: Paul Chapman.

Inner London Education Authority (ILEA) (1990) *A Curriculum for Young Children: Outdoor Play*. London: Harcourt Brace Jovanovich.

Isaacs, S. (1968) *The Nursery Years*. London: Routledge and Kegan Paul.

Jones, N. (1989) Preface, in G. Barrett (ed.), *Disaffection from School? The Early Years*. Lewes: Falmer Press.

Jones, P. (1988) *Lipservice: The Story of Talk in Schools*. Milton Keynes: Open University Press.

Kagan, S. (1988) *Cooperative Learning: Resources for Teachers*. Riverside, CA: University of California.

Kimberley, K. (1990) The third limb: assessment and the national curriculum, *The English Magazine*, **23** (Summer): 19–26.

Lee, L. (1959) *Cider with Rosie*. London: Hogarth Press.

Lindon, J. (1993) *Child Development from Birth to Eight*. London: National Children's Bureau.

Manning, K. and Sharp, A. (1977) *Structuring Play in the Early Years at School*. London: Ward Lock International.

Meadows, S. (1993) *The Child as Thinker: The Development and Acquisition of Cognition in Childhood*. London: Routledge.

Meighan, J. (1993) The hijack of young children's learning, in R. Meighan (ed.), *Theory and Practice of Regressive Education*. Nottingham: Educational Heretics Press.

Mortimore, P., Sammons, P., Stoll, L. and Ecob, R. (1986) *The Junior School Project*. London: ILEA.

Moss, P. and Penn, H. (1996) *Transforming Nursery Education*. London: Paul Chapman.

Moyles, J.R. (1989) *Just Playing? The Role and Status of Play in Early Childhood Education*. Milton Keynes: Open University Press.

Moyles, J.R. (1992) *Organising for Learning in the Primary Classroom*. Milton Keynes: Open University Press.

National Commission on Education (1993) *Learning to Succeed*. London: Heinemann.

Nutbrown, C. (1994) *Threads of Thinking*. London: Paul Chapman.

Office for Standards in Education (Ofsted) (1991) *Well Managed Classes in Primary Schools: Case Studies of Six Teachers*. London: DFE.

Office for Standards in Education (Ofsted) (1993a) *Curriculum Organisation and Classroom Practice in Primary Schools: A Follow-up Report*. London: DFE.

Office for Standards in Education (Ofsted) (1993b) *First Class: The Standards and Quality of Education in Reception Classes*. London: HMSO.

Office for Standards in Education (Ofsted) (1994a) *Assessing School Effectiveness*. London: Institute of Education.

Office for Standards in Education (Ofsted) (1994b) *Primary Matters: A Discussion on Teaching and Learning in Primary Schools*. London: HMSO.

Osborn, M. and Pollard, A. with Abbott, D., Broadfoot, P. and Croll, P. (1991) Anxiety and paradox: Teachers' initial responses to change under the National Curriculum. *Working Paper No. 3*. Bristol: PACE.

Oxfordshire Early Years Team (1996) *Curriculum Matters 13: Early Years*. Oxfordshire Education Department.

Pascal, C. (1990) *Under-fives in the Infant Classroom*. Stoke-on-Trent: Trentham.

Pascal, C. and Ghaye, A. (1988) Four year old children in reception classrooms: Participant perceptions and practice, *Educational Studies*, **14**(2): 187–208.

Phillips, T. (1988) On a related matter: Why successful small-group talk depends upon not keeping to the point, in M. Maclure, T. Phillips and A. Wilkinson (eds), *Oracy Matters*. Milton Keynes: Open University Press.

Piaget, J. and Inhelder, B. (1956) *The Child's Conception of Space*. London: Routledge and Kegan Paul.

Pollard, A. and Tann, S. (1993) *Reflective Teaching in the Primary School*, 2nd edn. London: Cassell.

Pollard, A., Broadfoot, P., Croll, P., Osborn, M. and Abbott, D. (1994) *Changing English Primary Schools? The Impact of the Education Reform Act at Key Stage One*. London: Cassell.

Postlethwaite, K. (1993) *Differentiated Science Teaching*. Buckingham: Open University Press.

Pringle, M.K. (1992) *The Needs of Children*, 3rd edn. London: Routledge.

Rabain-Jamin, J. (1989) Culture and early social interactions. The example of mother–infant object play in African and native French families, *European Journal of Psychology of Education*, **4**(2): 295–305.

Reid, J., Forrestal, P. and Cook, J. (1989) *Small Group Learning in the Classroom*. Scarborough, WA: Chalkface Press.

Richards, M. and Light, P. (1986) *Children of Social Worlds*. Cambridge: Polity Press.

Roberts, R. (1995a) *Self Esteem and Successful Early Learning*. London: Hodder and Stoughton.

Roberts, R. (ed.) (1995b) *A Nursery Education Curriculum for the Early Years*. Oxford: National Primary Centre.

Rousseau, J.J. (1762/1963) *Emile*. (translated by Barbara Foxley). London: Dent.

Rowland, S. (1984) *The Enquiring Classroom: An Introduction to Children's Learning*. Lewes: Falmer Press.

Rubin, K., Fein, G. and Vandenberg, B. (1983) Play, in E.M. Hetherington (ed.), *Manual of Child Psychology: Socialization, Personality and Development*, Vol. IV. New York: John Wiley.

Schön, D.A. (1987) *Educating the Reflective Practitioner*. San Francisco, CA: Jossey-Bass.

School Curriculum and Assessment Authority (SCAA) (1995) *Planning the Curriculum at Key Stages 1 and 2*. London: SCAA.

School Curriculum and Assessment Authority (SCAA) (1996) *Consultation Paper on Baseline Assessment*. London: SCAA.

School Curriculum and Assessment Authority (SCAA) (1996) *Desirable Outcomes for Children's Learning on Entering Compulsory Education*. London: SCAA.

Schweinhart, L.J., Barnes, H. and Weikart, D.P. (1993) *Significant Benefits: The High/Scope Perry Preschool Study through Age 27*. Ypsilanti, MI: High/Scope Press.

Sestini, E. (1987) The quality of the learning experiences of four year olds in nursery and infant classes, in *Four Year Olds in School* (NFER/SCDC Seminar Report). Slough: NFER.

Shaffer, D.R. (1993) *Developmental Psychology: Childhood and Adolescence*, 3rd edn. Pacific Grove, CA: Brooks/Cole.

Sinclair, J. McH. and Coulthard, R.M. (1975) *Towards an Analysis of Discourse: The English Used by Teachers and Pupils*. London: Oxford University Press.

Smith, A.B. (1993) Early childhood educare: Seeking a theoretical framework in Vygotsky's work, *International Journal of Early Years Education*, **1**(1): 47–61.

Smith, P.K. and Cowie, H. (1991) *Understanding Children's Development*, 2nd edn. Oxford: Blackwell.

Spender, D. (1982) *Invisible Women: The Schooling Scandal*. London: Writers and Readers.

Stanworth, M. (1981) *Gender and Schooling: A Study of Gender Divisions in the Classroom*. London: Women's Research and Resources Centre.

Stern, D. (1985) *The Interpersonal World of the Infant: A View from Psychoanalysis and Developmental Psychology*. New York: Basic Books.

Stevenson, C. (1987) The young four-year-old in nursery and infant classes: Challenges and constraints, in *Four Year Olds in School* (NFER/SCDC Seminar Report). London: NFER/SCDC.

Stodolsky, S.S., Ferguson, T.L. and Wimpelberg, K. (1981) The recitation persists; but what does it look like?, *Journal of Curriculum Studies*, **13**: 121–30.

Sutton-Smith, B. and Kelly-Byrne, D. (1984) The idealization of play, in P.K. Smith (ed.), *Play in Animals and Humans*. Oxford: Blackwell.

Sylva, K. (1994) The impact of early learning on children's later development, Appendix C, in C. Ball, *Start Right: The Importance of Early Learning*. London: RSA.

Sylva, K. and Lunt, I. (1982) *Child Development: A First Course*. Oxford: Blackwell.

Thomas, I. (1987) The Bedfordshire 4+ pilot scheme: Some issues and implications, in *Four Year Olds in School* (NFER/SCDC Seminar Report). Slough: NFER.

Tizard, B. and Hughes, M. (1984) *Young Children Learning: Talking and Thinking at Home and at School*. London: Fontana.

Tizard, B., Blatchford, D., Burke, J., Farquar, C. and Plewis, I. (1988) *Young Children at School in the Inner City*. Hove: Lawrence Erlbaum Associates.

Tompkins, M. (1991) In praise of praising less, *Extensions* (Newsletter of the High/Scope Curriculum), **6**(1): 1–3.

Vygotsky, L.S. (1962) *Thought and Language*. Cambridge, MA: MIT Press.

Vygotsky, L.S. (1966) Play and its role in the mental development of the child (translated by Catherine Mulholland), in *Voprosy psikhologi*, **12**(6): 62–76.

Vygotsky, L.S. (1978) *Mind in Society: The Development of Higher Psychological Processes*. Cambridge, MA: Harvard University Press.

Warham, S.M. (1993) *Primary Teaching and the Negotiation of Power*. London: Paul Chapman.

Watson, R. (1996) Rethinking readiness for learning, in D. Olson and N. Torrance (eds), *The Handbook of Education and Human Development: New Models of Learning, Teaching and Schooling*. Oxford: Blackwell.

Wells, G. (ed.) (1981) *Learning through Interaction*. Cambridge: Cambridge University Press.

Wells, G. (1985) *Language, Learning and Education*. Windsor: NFER/Nelson.

Wells, G. (1986) *The Meaning Makers: Children Learning Language and Using Language to Learn*. Sevenoaks: Hodder and Stoughton.

Whitehead, M. (1992) Assessment at Key Stage 1: Core subjects and the developmental curriculum, in G.M. Blenkin and A.V. Kelly (eds), *Assessment in Early Childhood Education*. London: Paul Chapman.

Whitehead, M. (1993) Why not happiness? Reflections on change and conflict in early childhood education, in P. Gammage and J. Meighan (eds), *Early Childhood Education: Taking Stock*. Ticknall: Education Now Publishing.

Wilkinson, A.M. (1965) *Spoken English*. Educational Review Occasional Publications, no. 2, University of Birmingham School of Education.

Willes, M.J. (1983) *Children into Pupils: A Study of Language in Early Schooling*. London: Routledge and Kegan Paul.

Wolfendale, S. (1993) *Baseline Assessment: A Review of Current Practice, Issues and Strategies for Effective Implementation*. Stoke-on-Trent: Trentham.

Wood, D. (1988) *How Children Think and Learn*. Oxford: Blackwell.

Wood, D., Bruner, J.S. and Ross, G. (1976) The role of tutoring in problem solving, *Journal of Child Psychology and Psychiatry*, **17**(2): 89–100.

Woods, P. (1990) *Teacher Skills and Strategies*. Basingstoke: Falmer Press.

INDEX

A NATIONAL CURRICULUM FOR THE EARLY YEARS

Angela Anning (ed.)

- What does the National Curriculum mean to pupils and teachers at Key Stage One?
- How have teachers and children coped with the ongoing changes?
- How has subject teaching altered in infant classrooms?

In *A National Curriculum for the Early Years*, Angela Anning and her team of contributors set out to examine these issues. Infant teachers and their pupils were the guinea pigs for the introduction of the National Curriculum over a five-year period. Despite many reservations about a subject-based curriculum for young children, teachers struggled to interpret the National Curriculum Orders into a workable, if not manageable, curriculum in their classrooms.

The contributors to this book, each experts in a subject discipline, have kept in close touch with practising and intending infant teachers as the National Curriculum was operationalized in primary schools. They have used their teacher networks, as well as research evidence, to tap into the strategies used by infant teachers to cope with the planning, delivery and assessment of the National Curriculum subjects and the effects of government policy changes on young children's learning.

Together the contributors provide a timely analysis of subject discipline based education for young children and look ahead to the prospects for those subjects at Key Stage One in the second half of the 1990s.

This book will be essential reading for anyone involved in the education of young children.

Contents
A national curriculum for key stage one – English – Mathematics – Science – Design and technology and information technology – Geography – History – Art – Music – Physical education – Religious education – The way ahead: Another national curriculum for key stage one? – Author index – Subject index.

Contributors
Angela Anning, Hilary Asoko, Roger Beard, Eileen Bellett, Helen Constable, David Dawson, Carolyn Jones, Ann MacNamara, Elizabeth Wood, Patrick Wiegand.

176pp   0 335 19431 1 (Paperback)   0 335 19432 X (Hardback)

QUALITY EDUCATION IN THE EARLY YEARS

Lesley Abbott and Rosemary Rodger (eds)

Lesley Abbott and her team of contributors identify and explore high
quality work (and what shapes it) in early years education. They show us
children and adults variously working and playing, talking and communicating, learning and laughing, caring and sharing in a rich tapestry
of case studies which highlight quality experiences and interactions.
Every chapter is based around a particular case study, each one tackling a
different issue: the curriculum, play, assessment, roles and relationships,
special needs, partnerships with parents, and equal opportunities.

All the writers work together in early years education on a day-to-day
basis enabling them to pool their different expertise to create a balanced
but challenging approach. They give inspiring examples of, and outline
underlying principles for, quality work and ask important questions of all
those involved in the education and care of young children.

Contents

*Introduction: The search for quality in the early years – A quality curriculum in
the early years: Raising some questions – 'Play is fun, but it's hard work too':
The search for quality play in the early years – 'Why involve me?' Encouraging
children and their parents to participate in the assessment process – 'It's nice
here now': Managing young children's behaviour – 'She'll have a go at anything': Towards an equal opportunities policy – 'We only speak English here,
don't we?' Supporting language development in a multilingual context – 'People
matter': The role of adults in providing a quality learning environment for the
early years – 'You feel like you belong': Establishing partnerships between parents and educators – 'Look at me – I'm only two': Educare for the under threes:
The importance of early experience – Looking to the future: Concluding comments – Bibliography – Index.*

Contributors

Lesley Abbott, Janet Ackers, Janice Adams, Caroline Barratt-Pugh, Brenda
Griffin, Chris Marsh, Sylvia Phillips, Rosemary Rodger, Helen Strahan.

224pp   0 335 19230 0 (Paperback)   0 335 19231 9 (Hardback)

EFFECTIVE EARLY YEARS EDUCATION
TEACHING YOUNG CHILDREN

Anne Edwards and Peter Knight

In this concise and accessible guide, the authors are sympathetic to the particular demands of teaching three to eight year olds and offer practical solutions to the complex issues that are currently faced by early years educators. In recognizing the demands on practitioners, they provide new and challenging frameworks for an understanding of the practice of teaching young children and draw upon international research to offer a sound model of early years subject-structured teaching which has the quality of children's learning at its centre. Their aim is to support teaching expertise through stimulating teachers' thinking about children's development, motivation, ways of learning and the subjects they teach. These topics are clearly set in the complex institutional settings in which practitioners work and ways of taking and evaluating action are offered.

Contents

176pp   0 335 19188 6 (Paperback)   0 335 19189 4 (Hardback)